PEACOCK
COLORING BOOK
FOR ADULTS

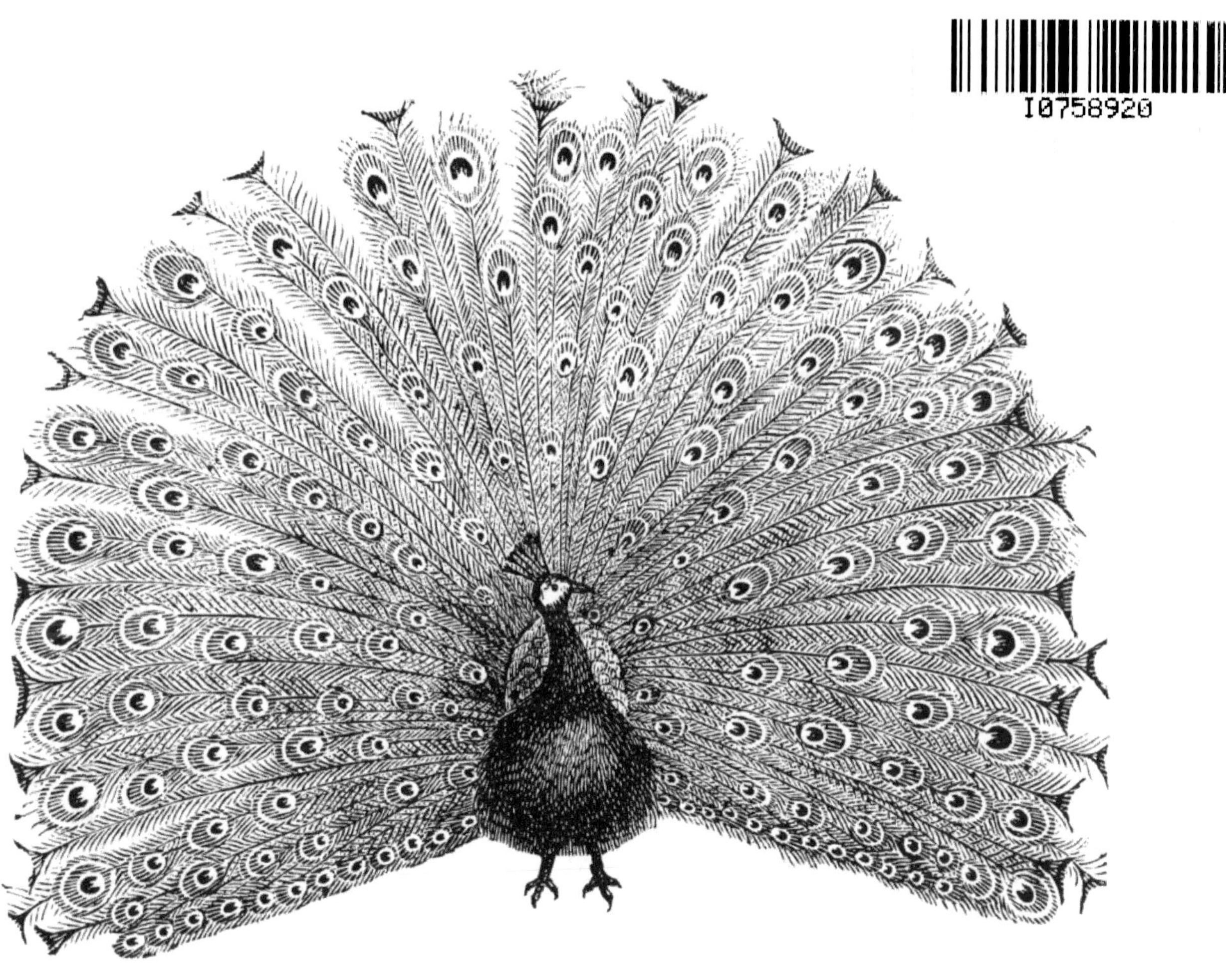

52 Peacock Coloring Pages

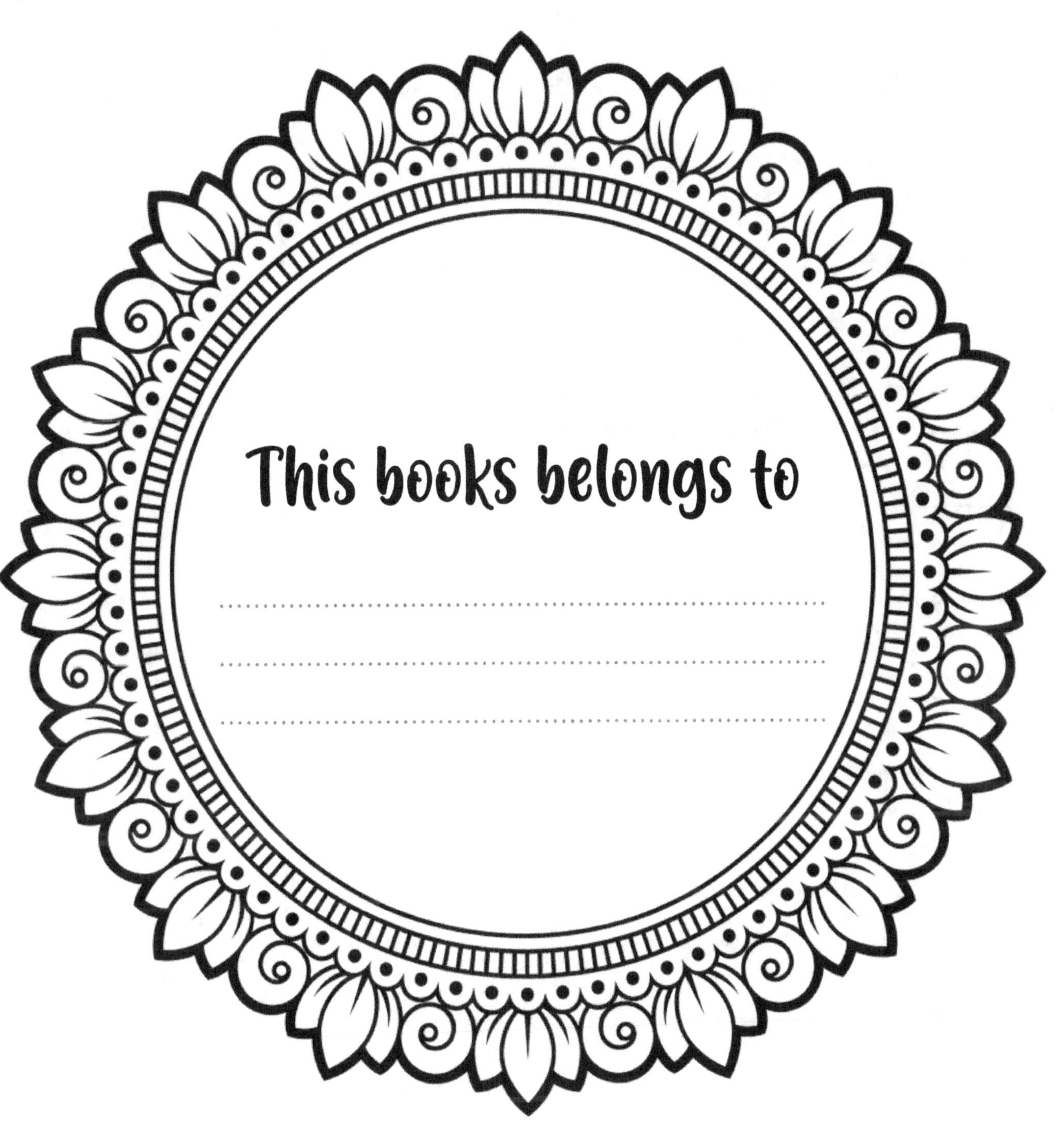
This books belongs to

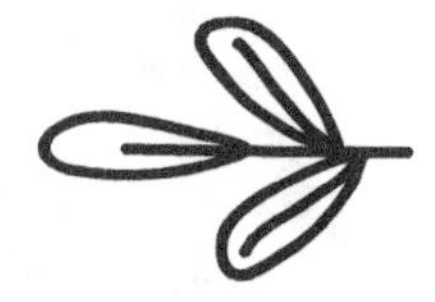 # Color Test Page 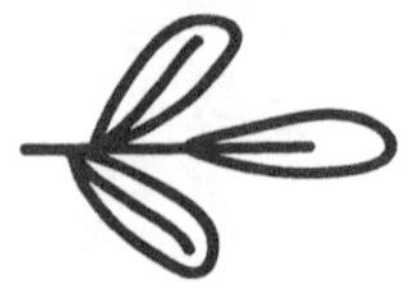

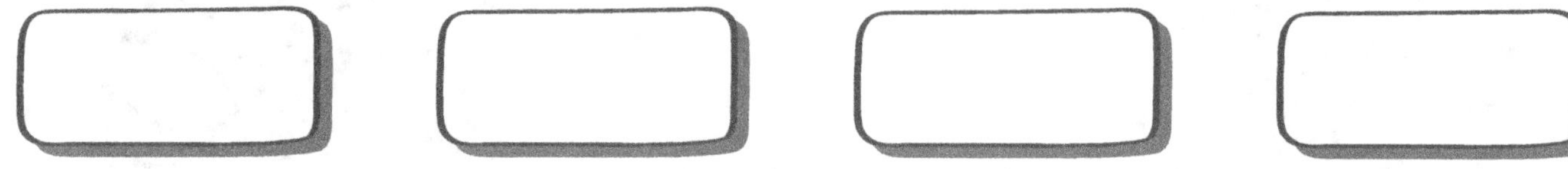
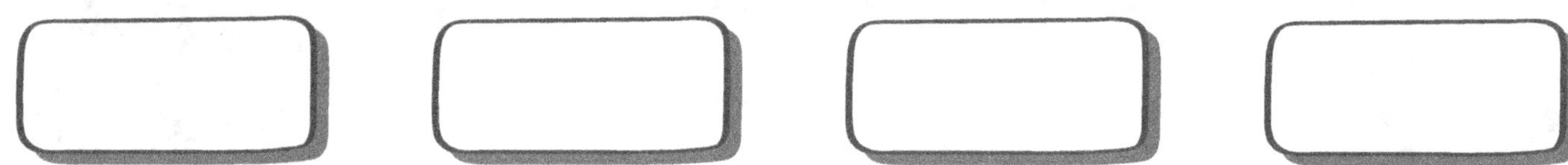
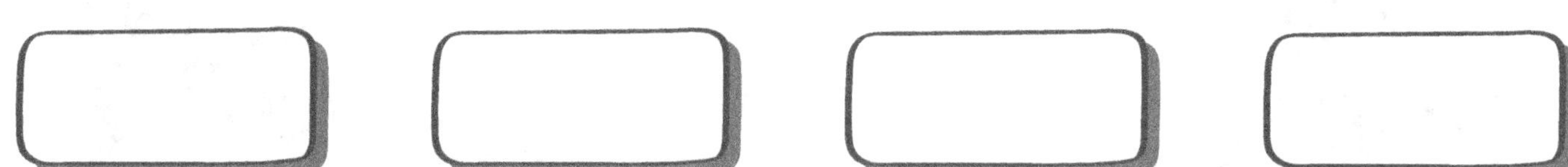
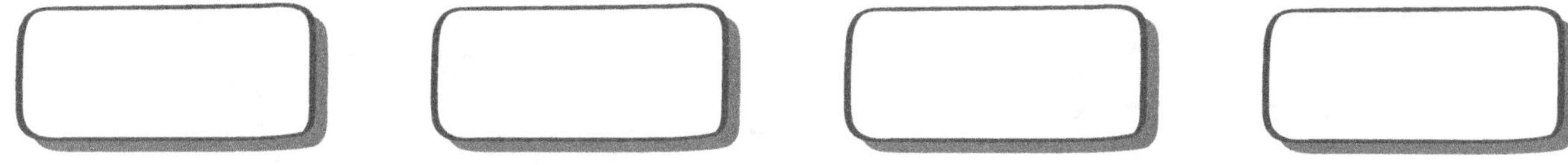
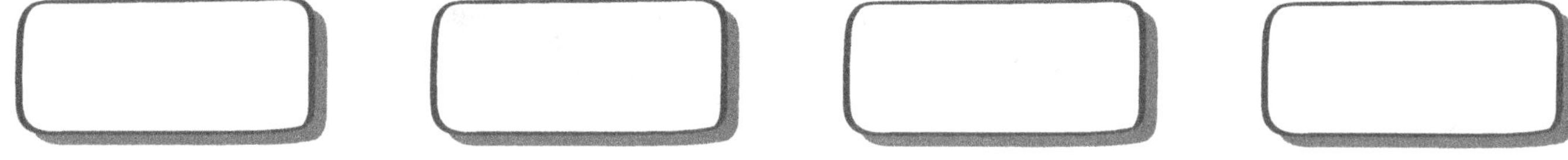
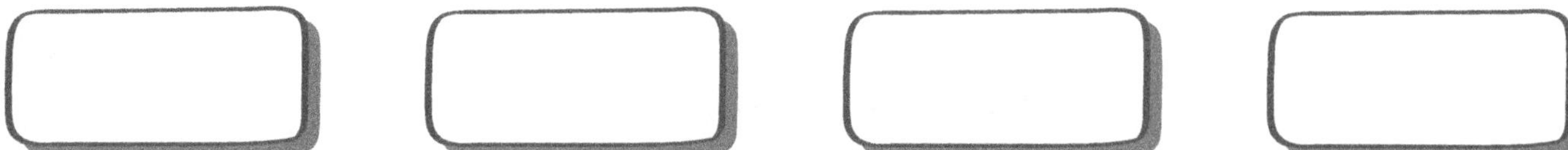

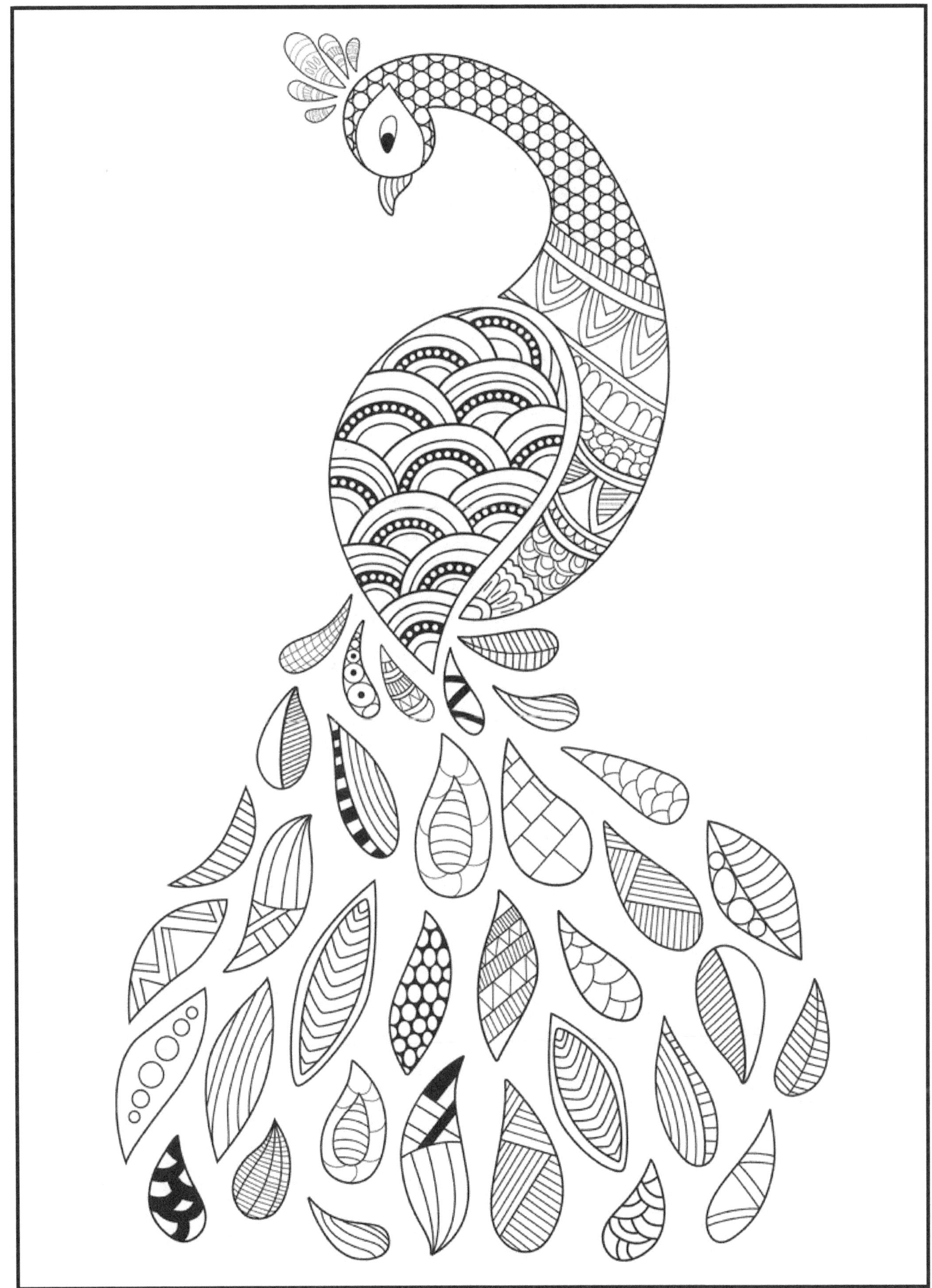

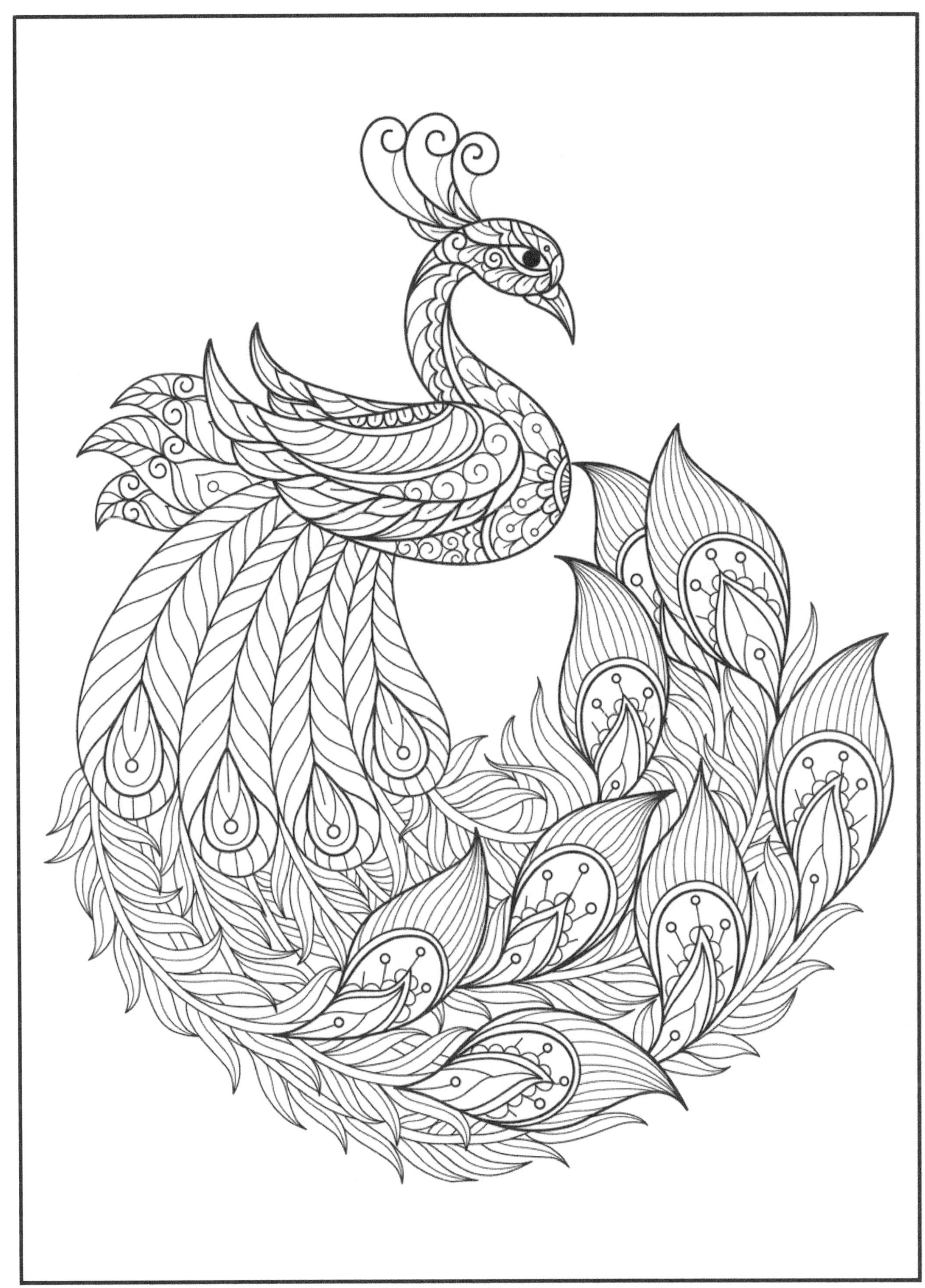

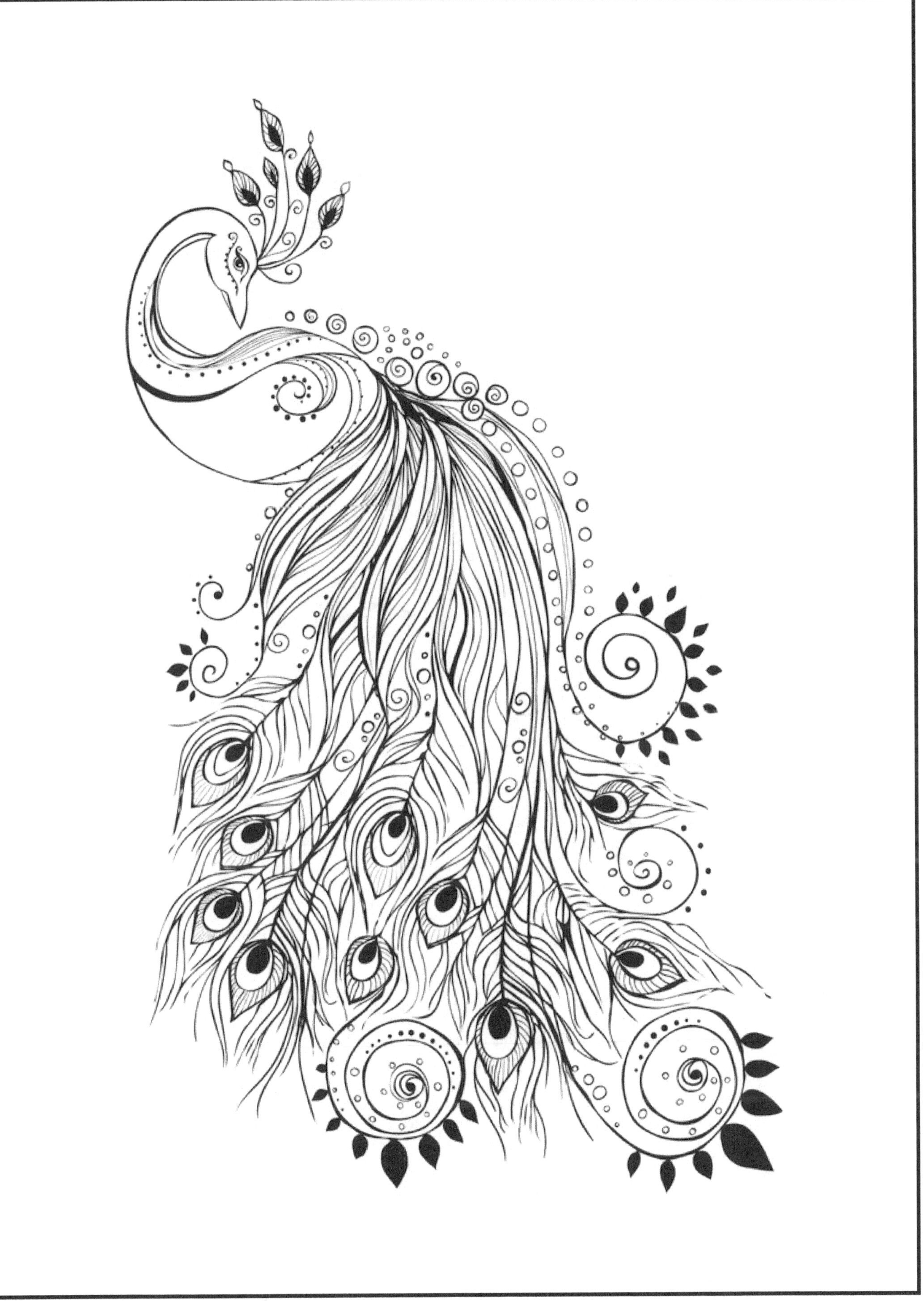

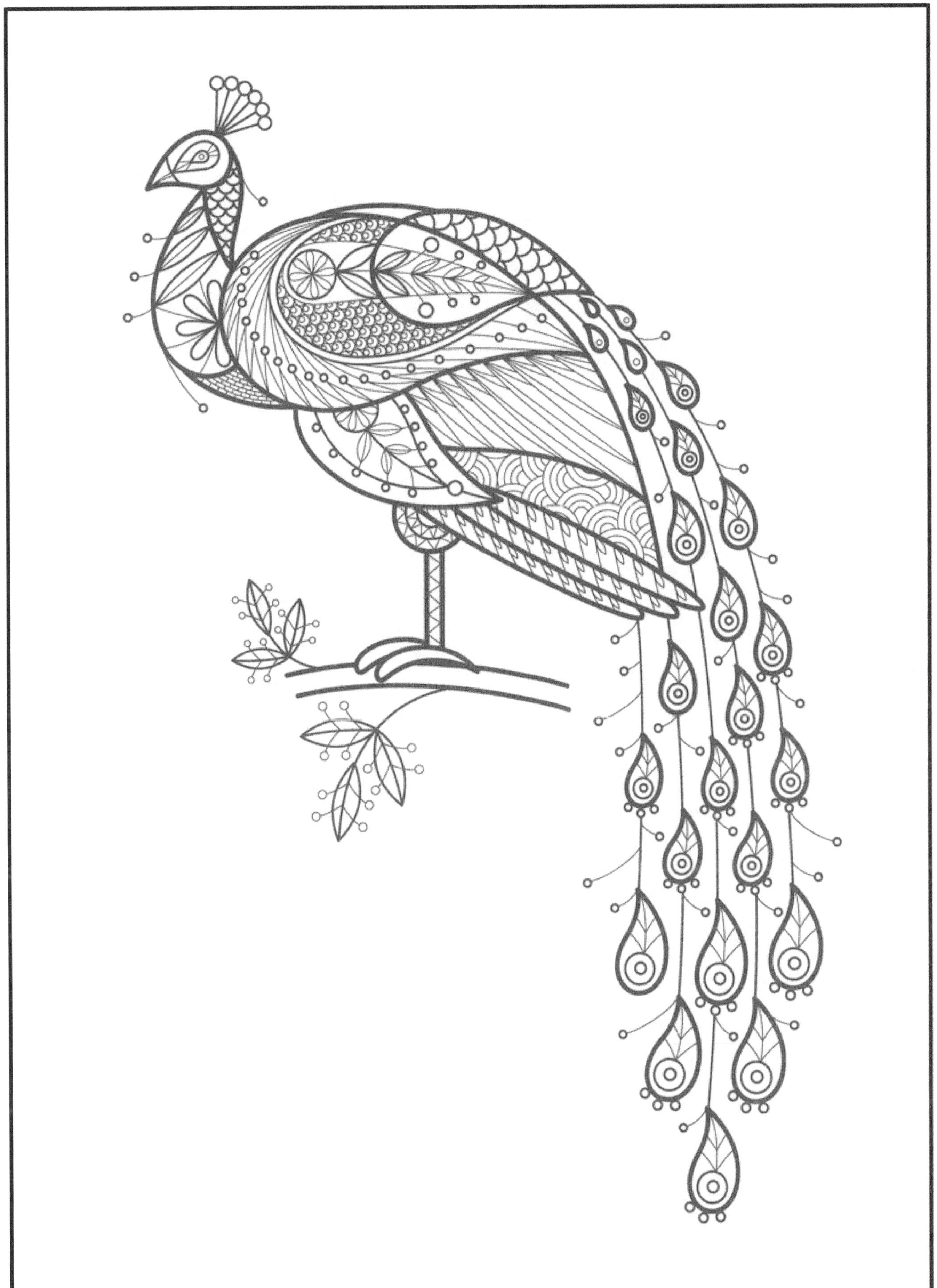

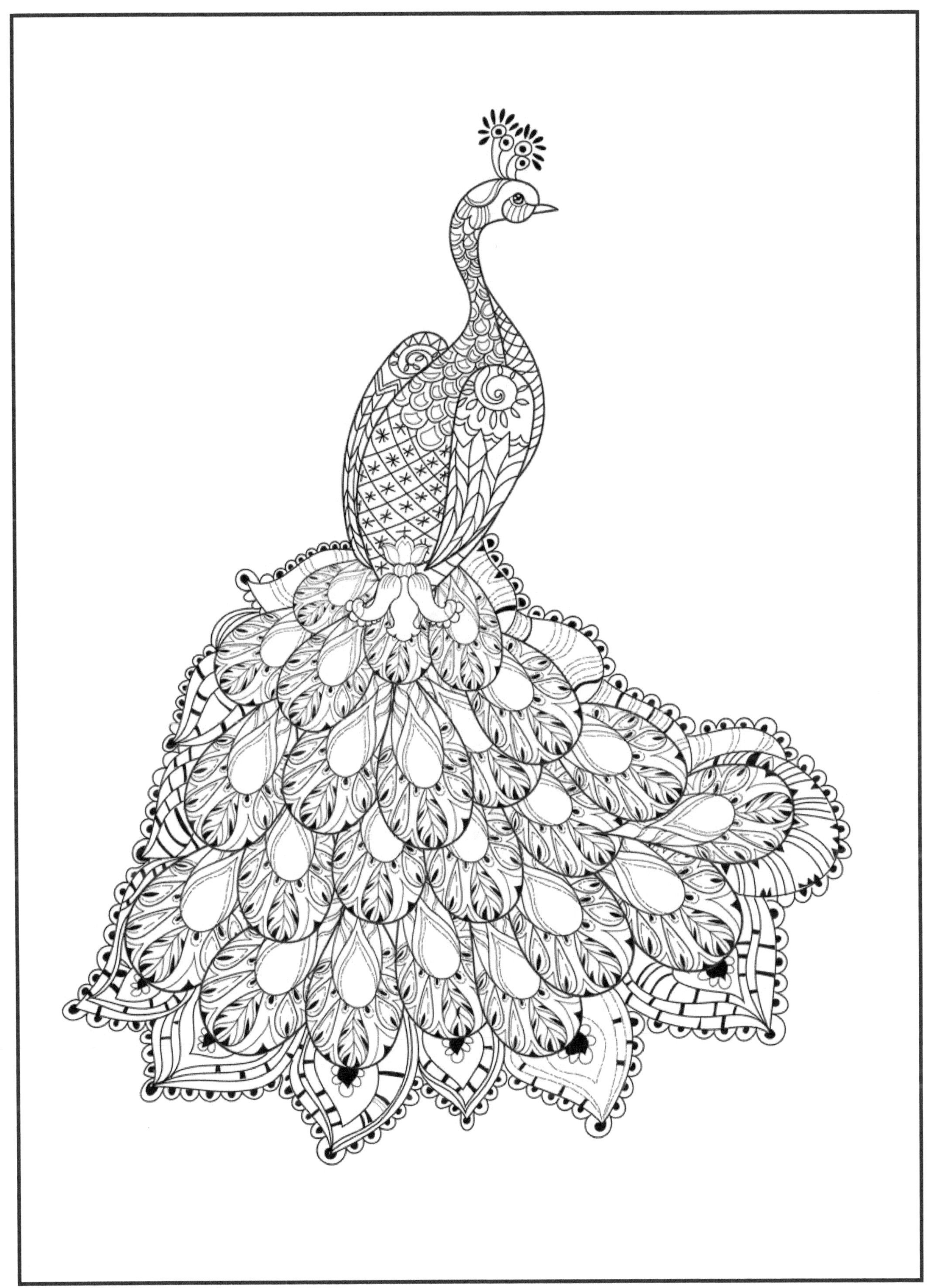

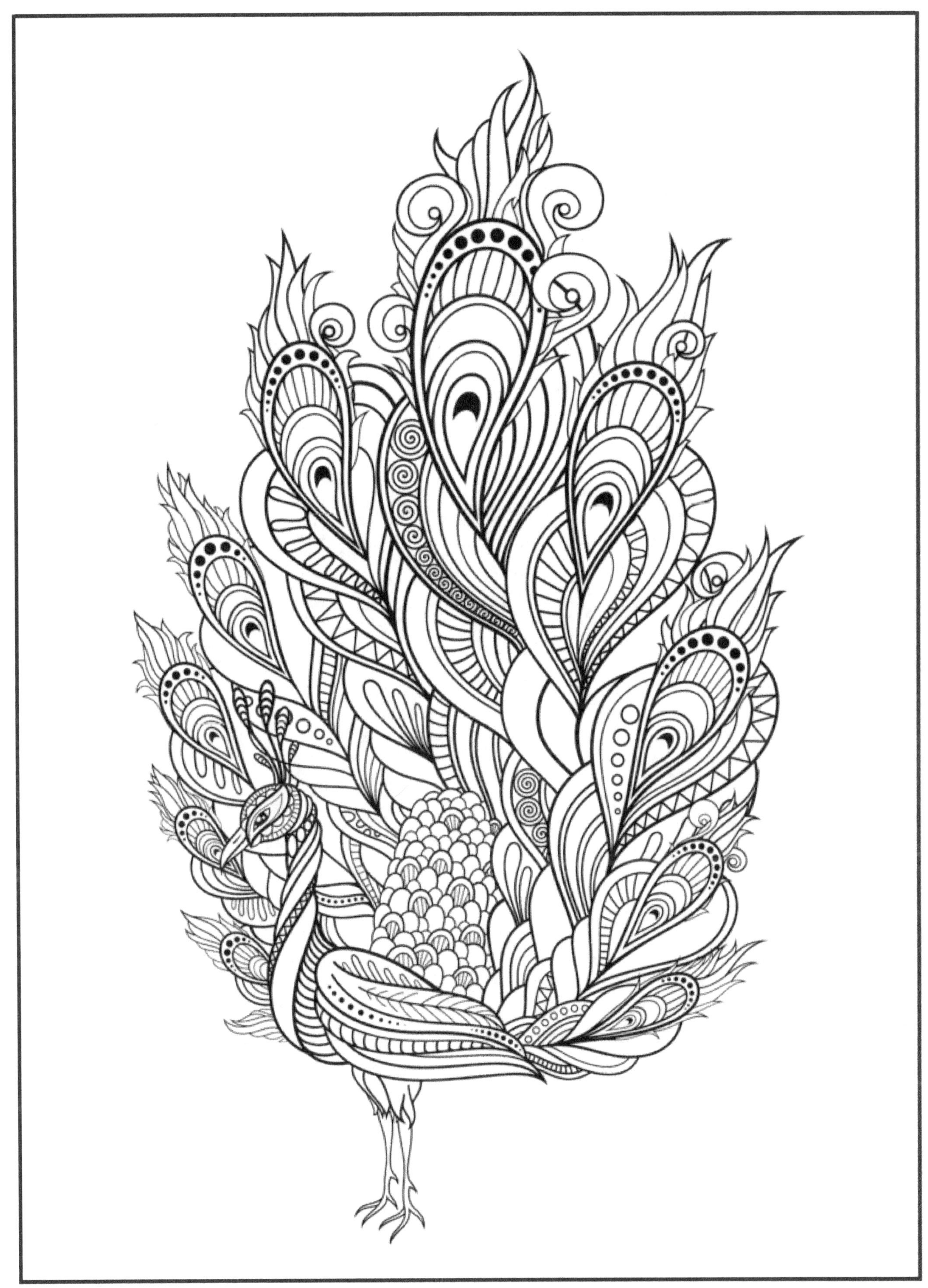

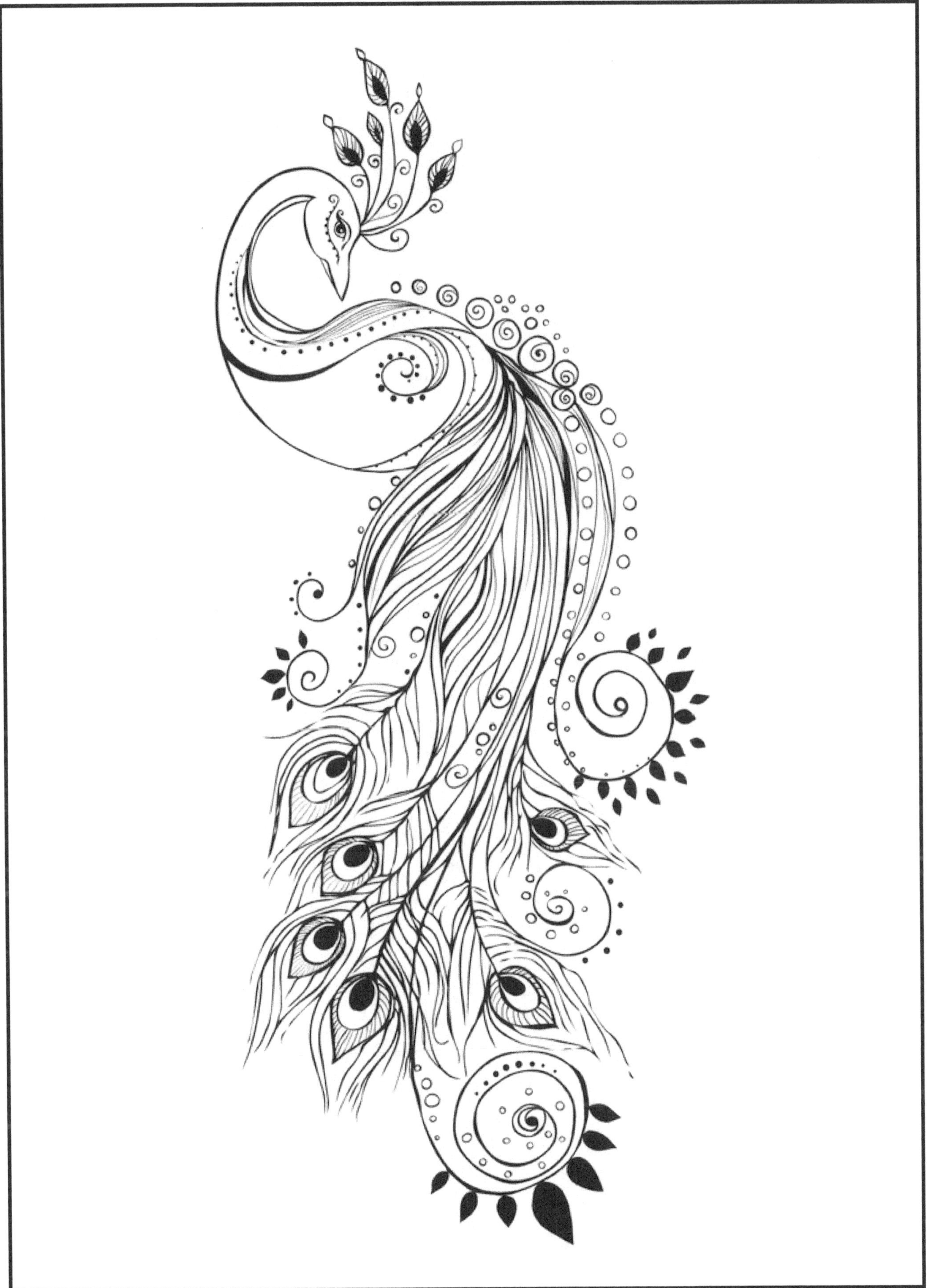

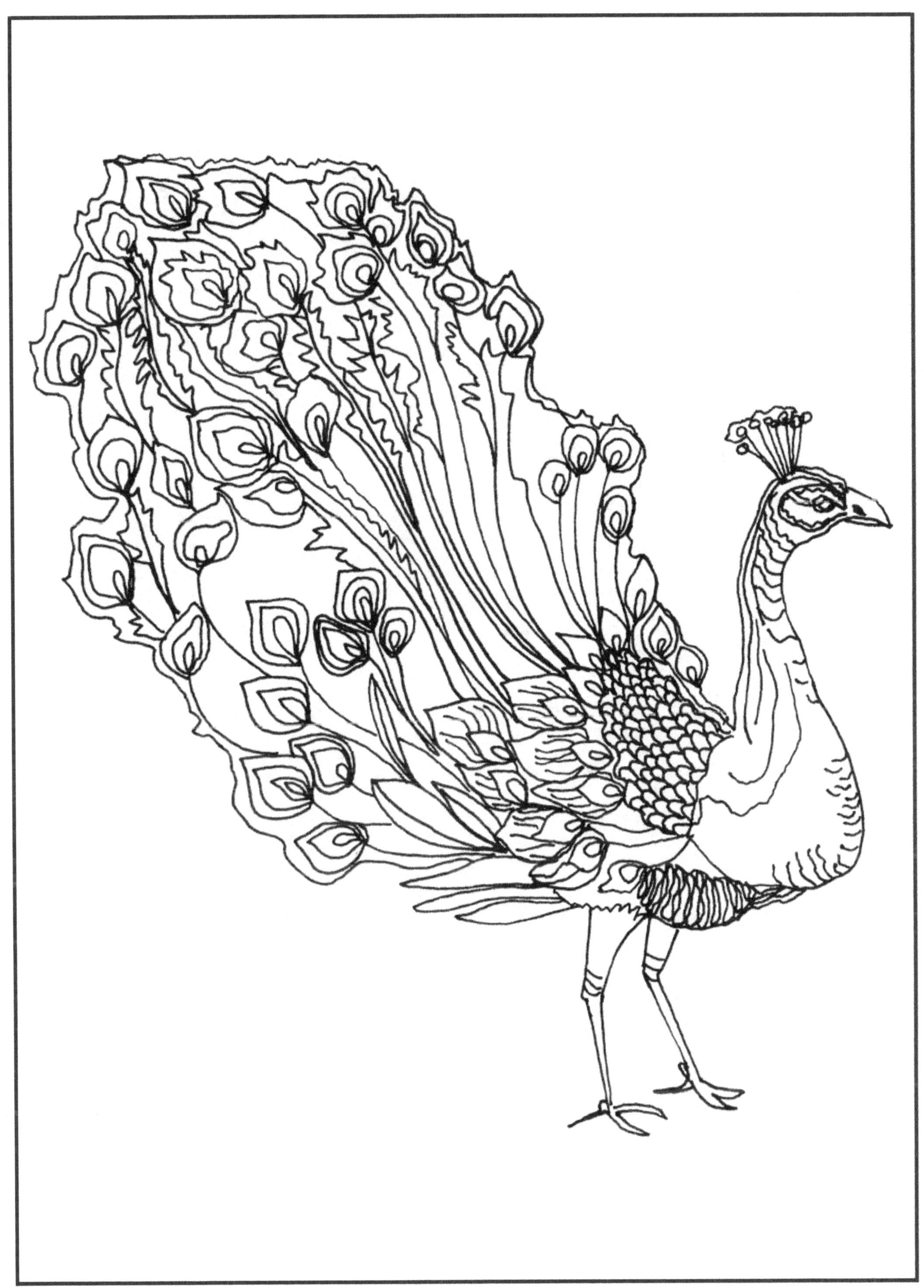

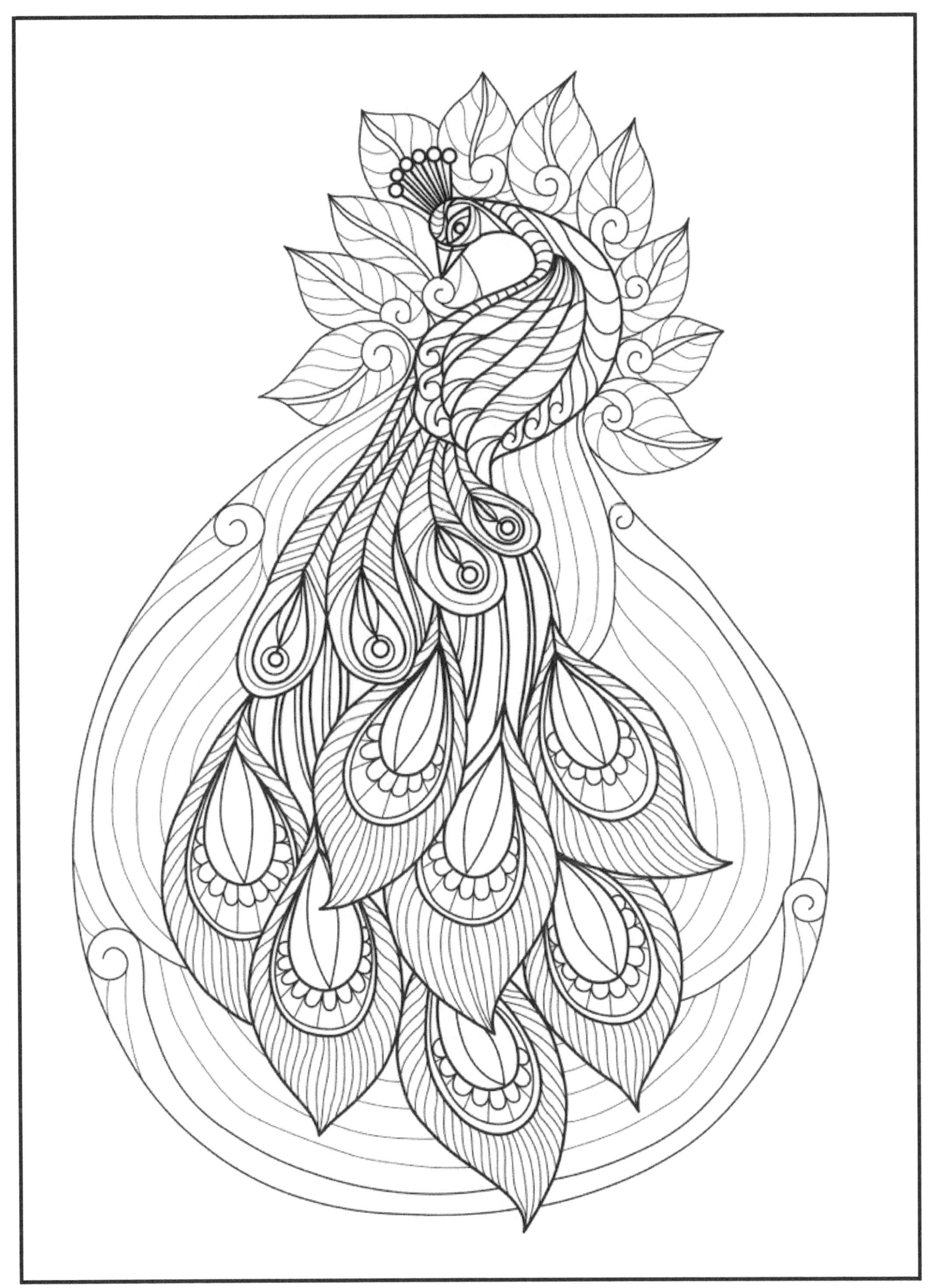

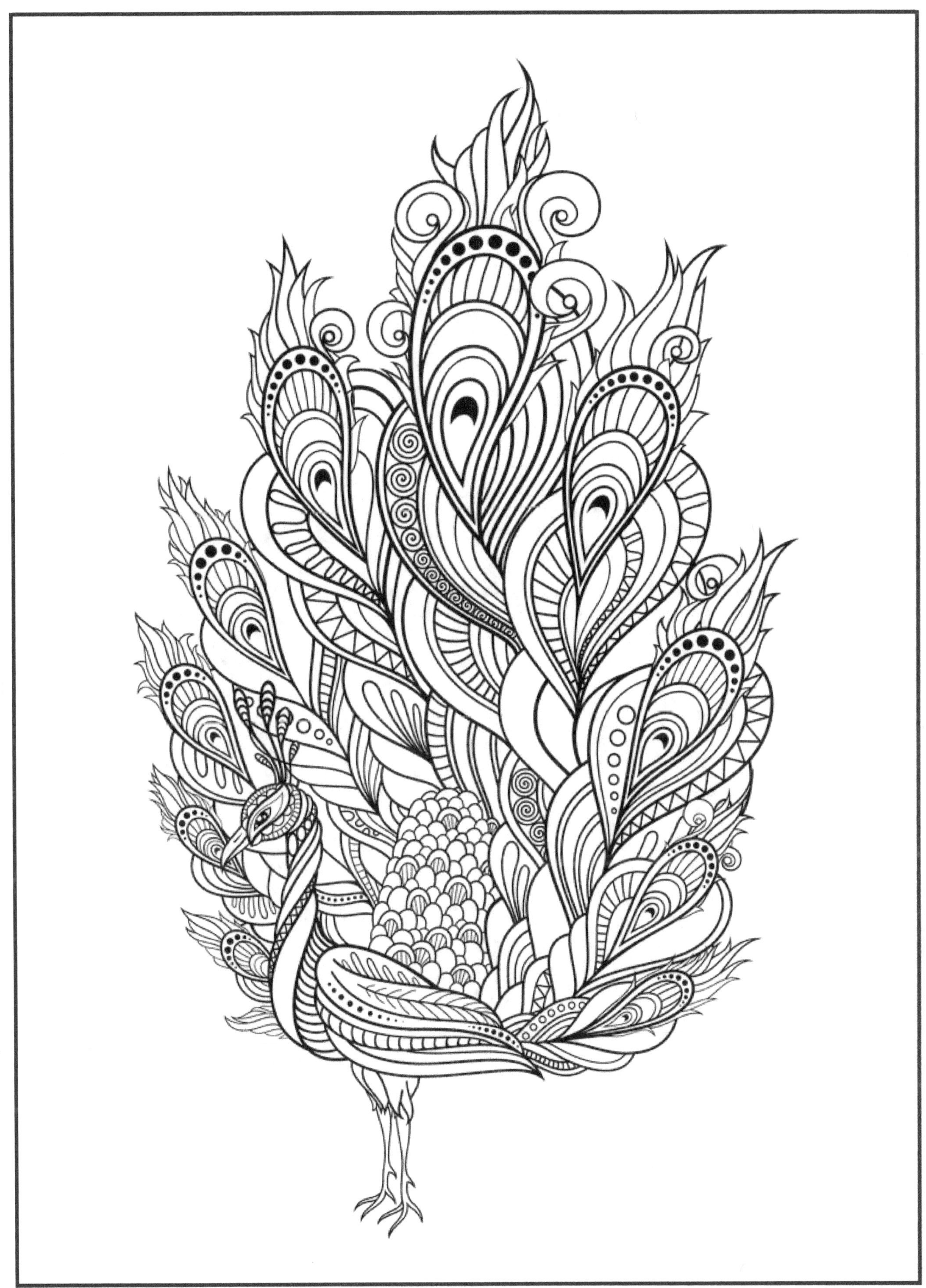

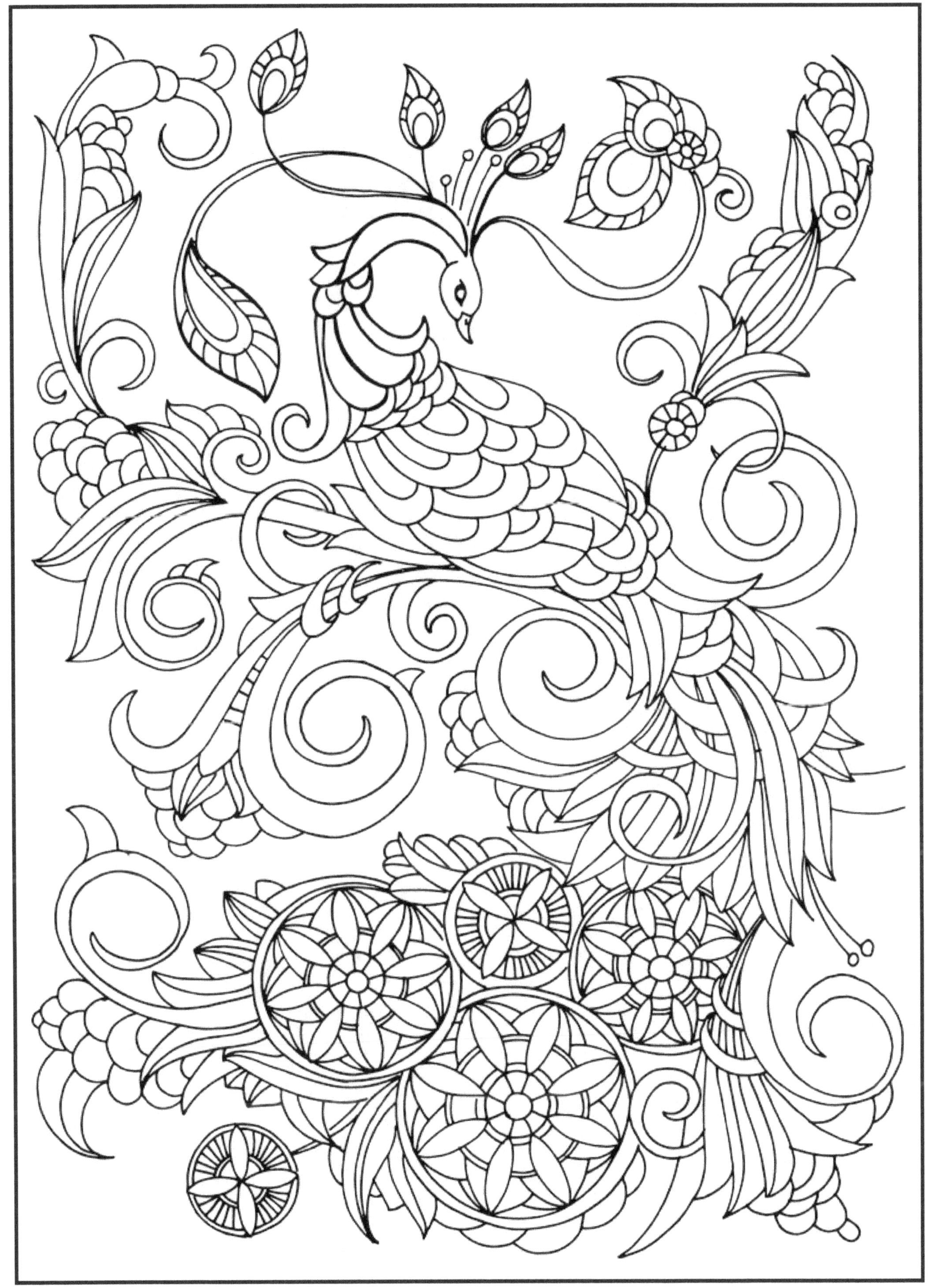

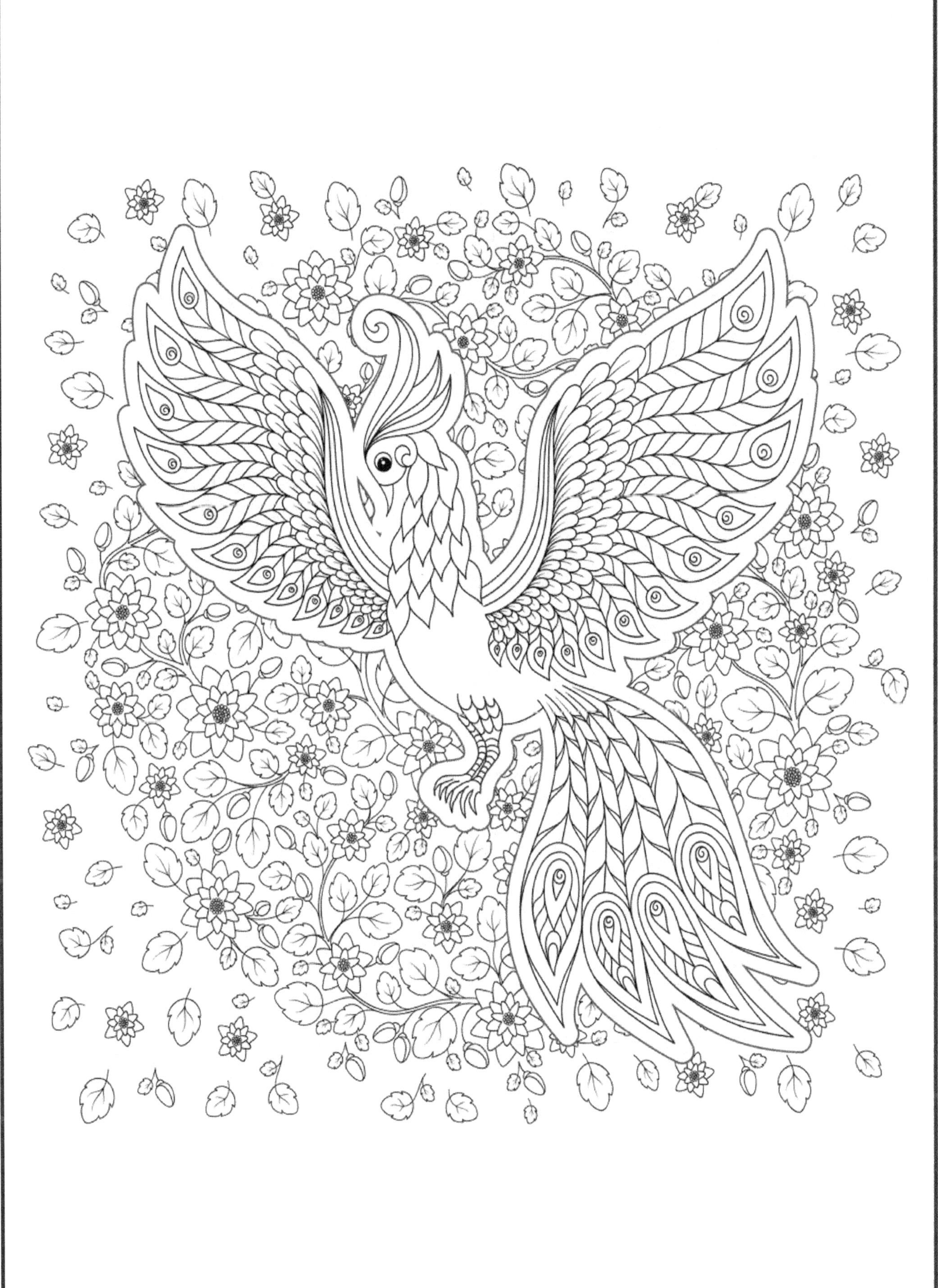

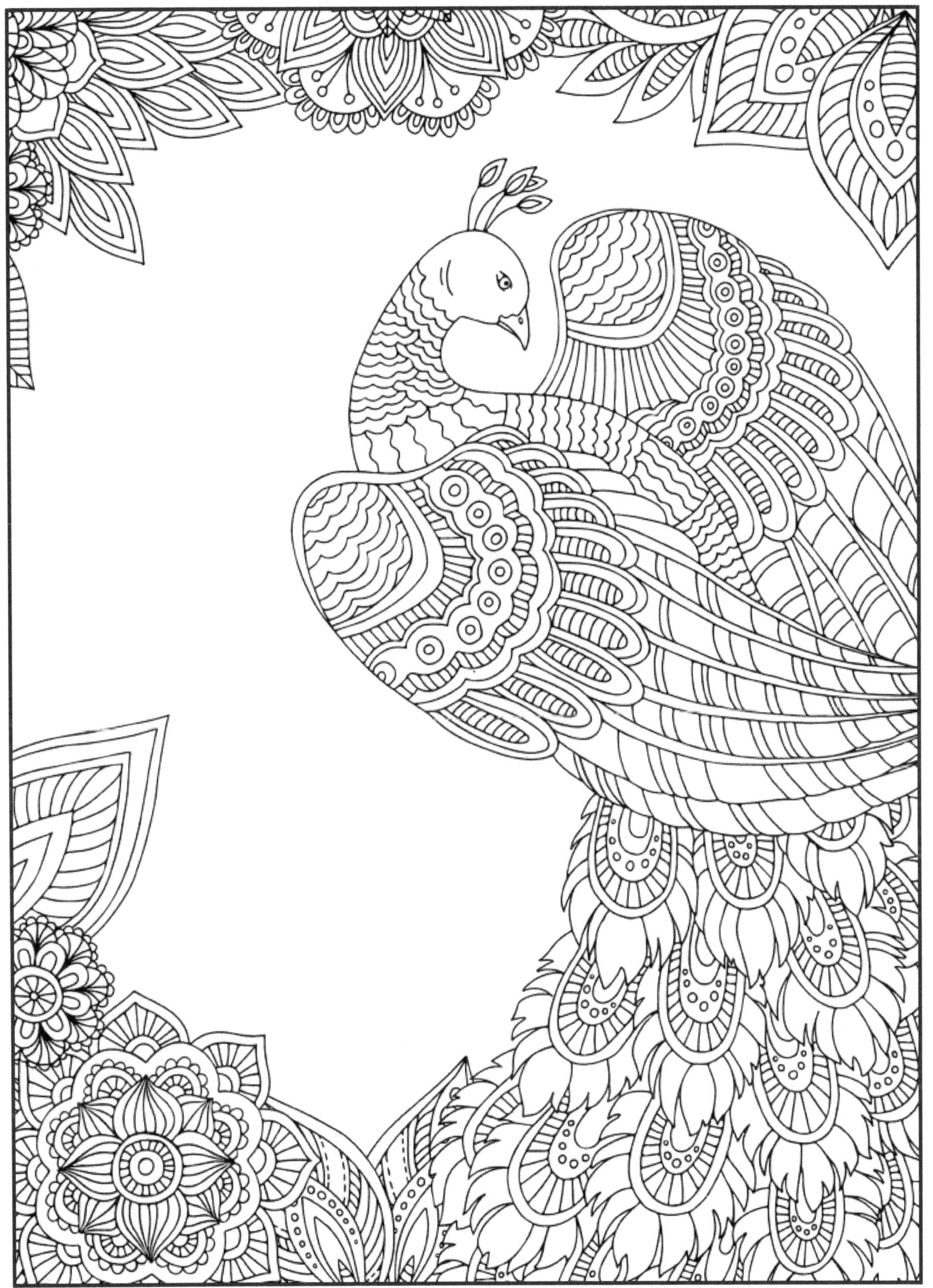

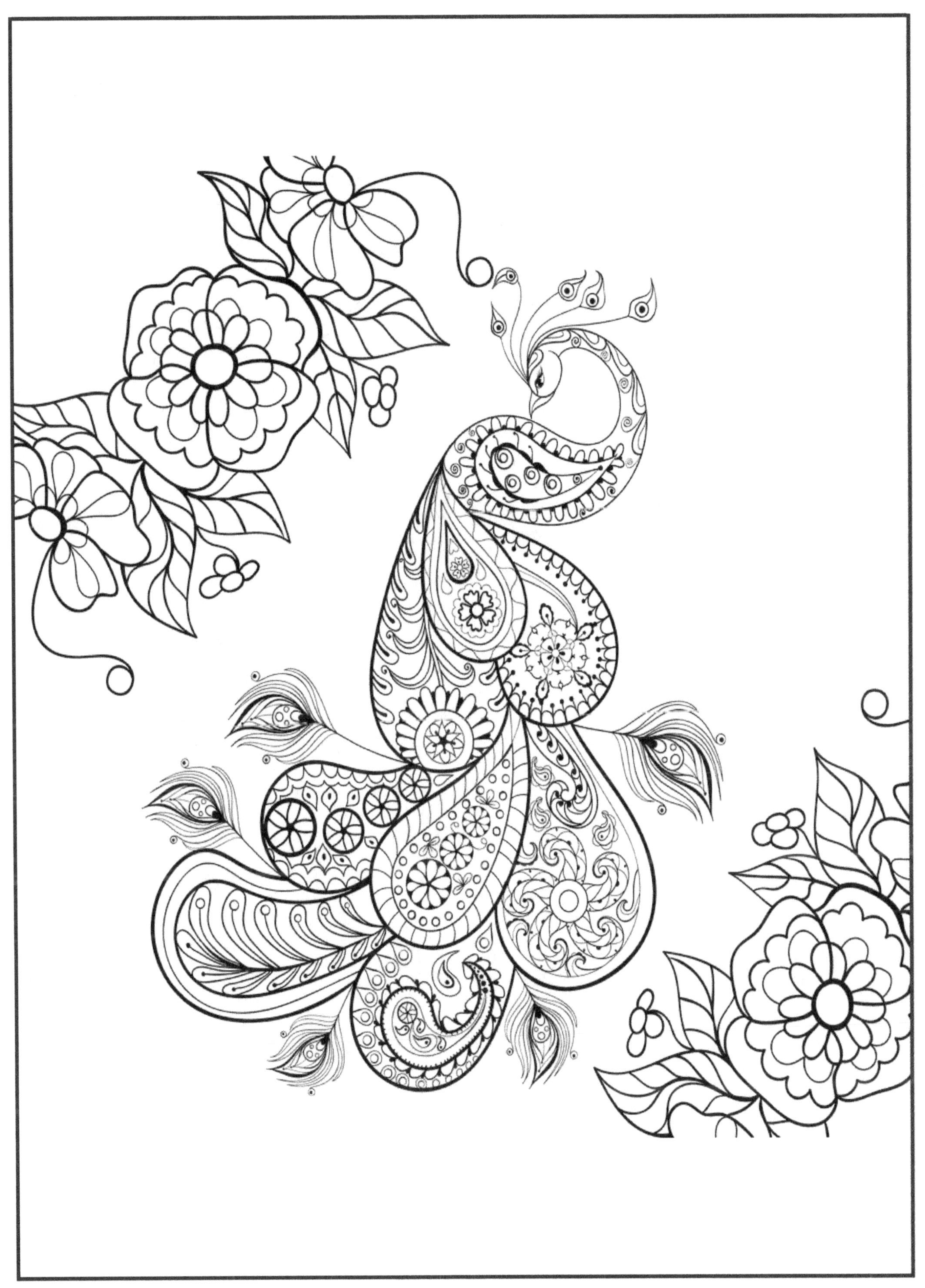

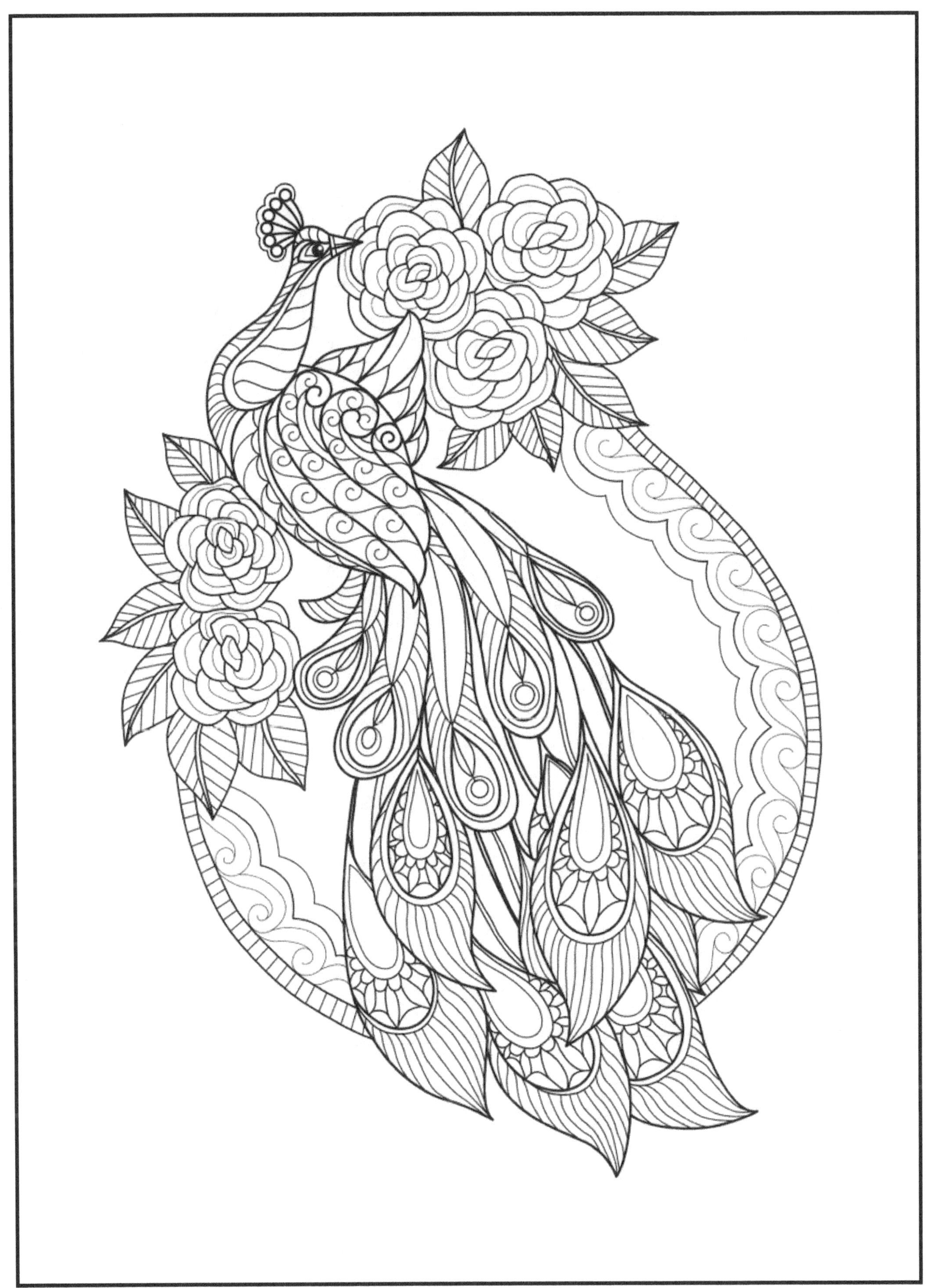

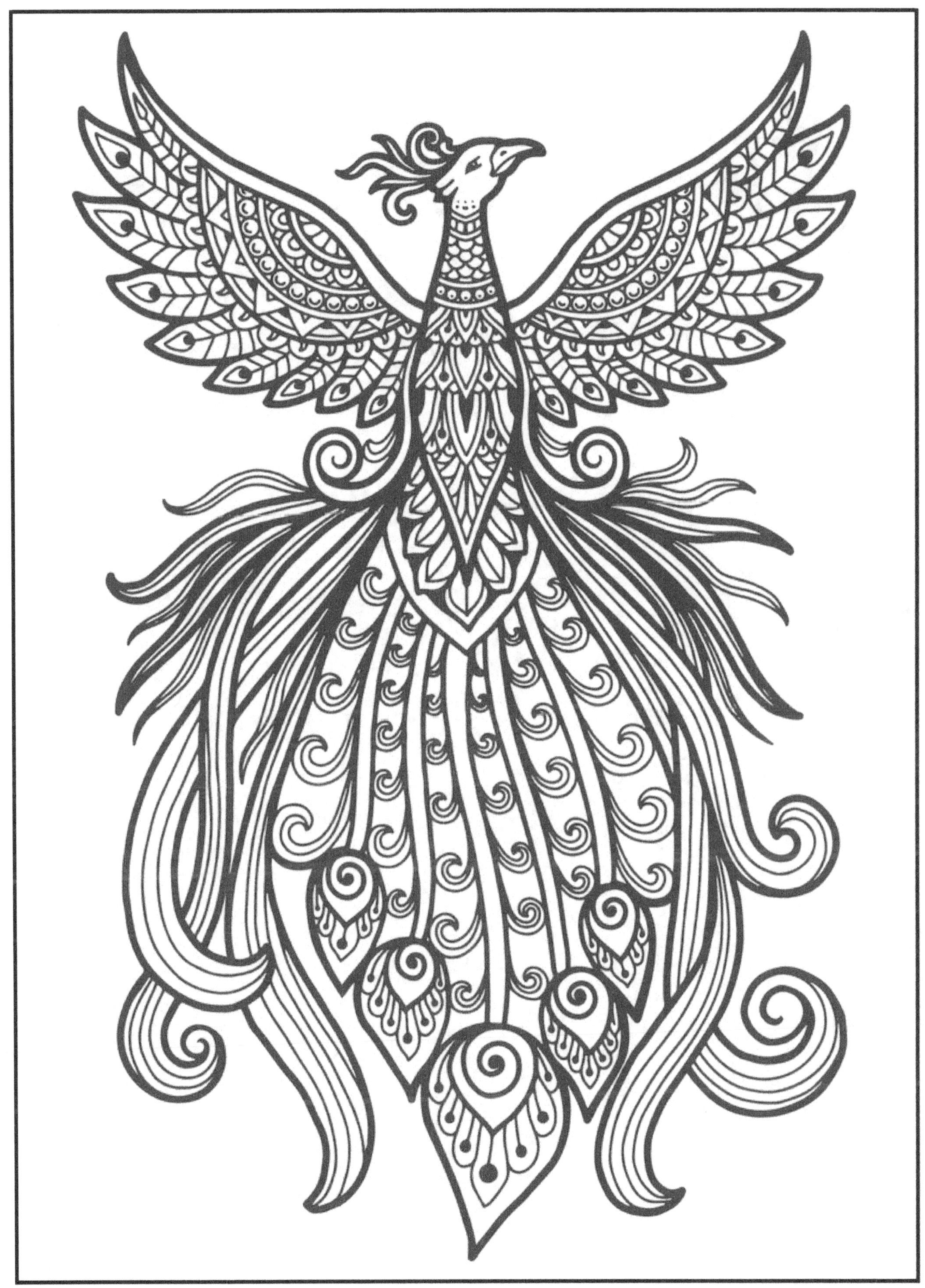

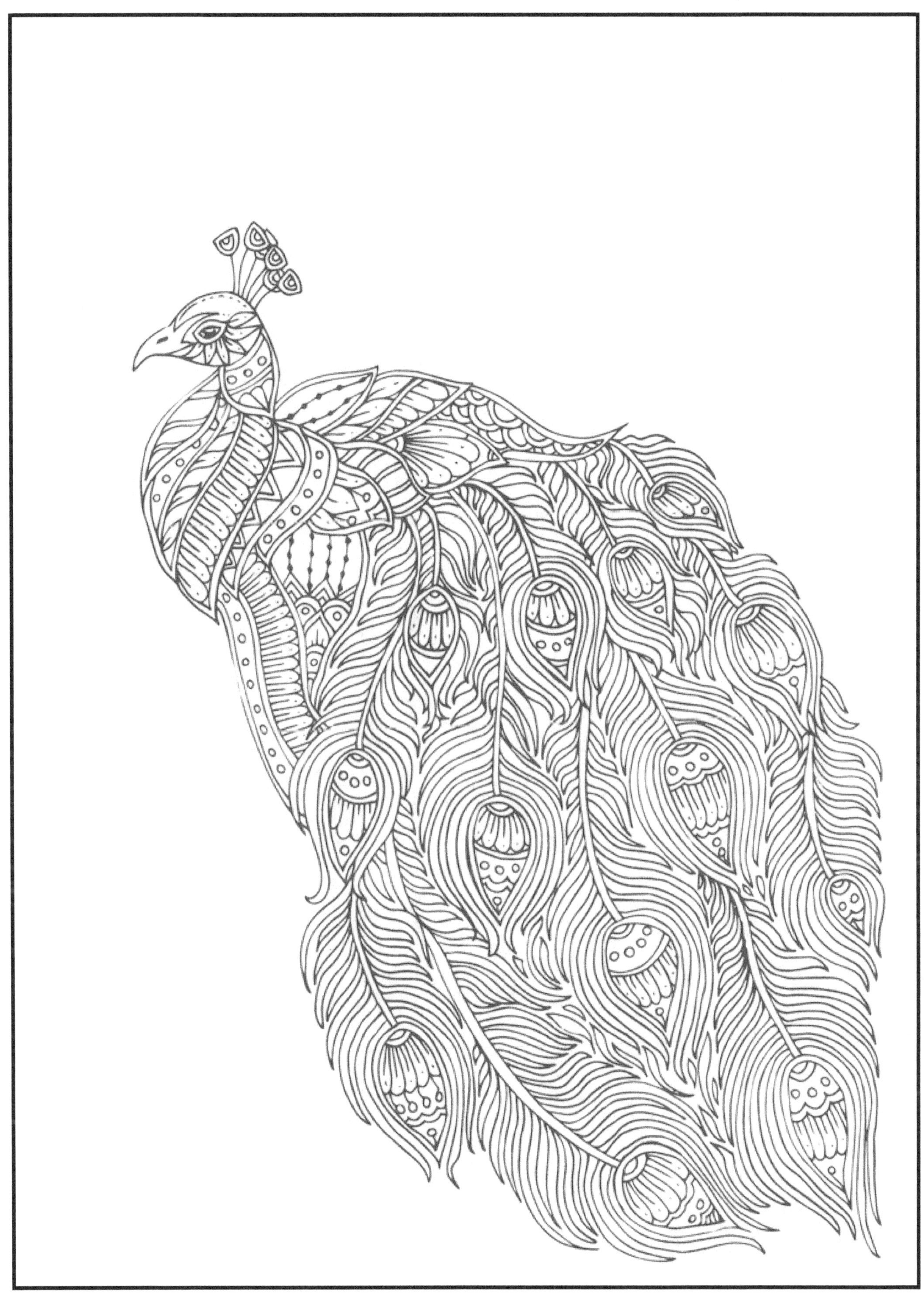

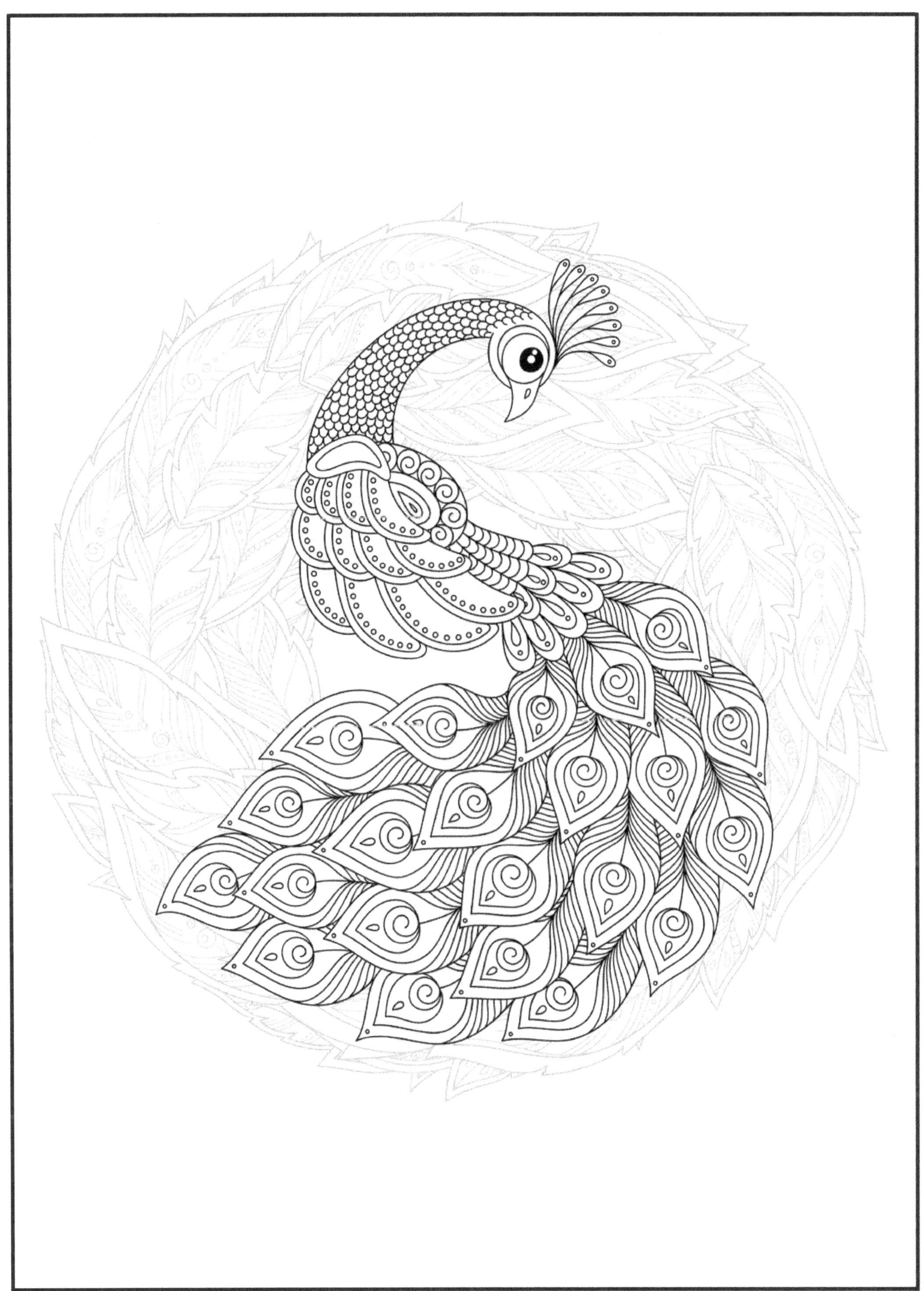

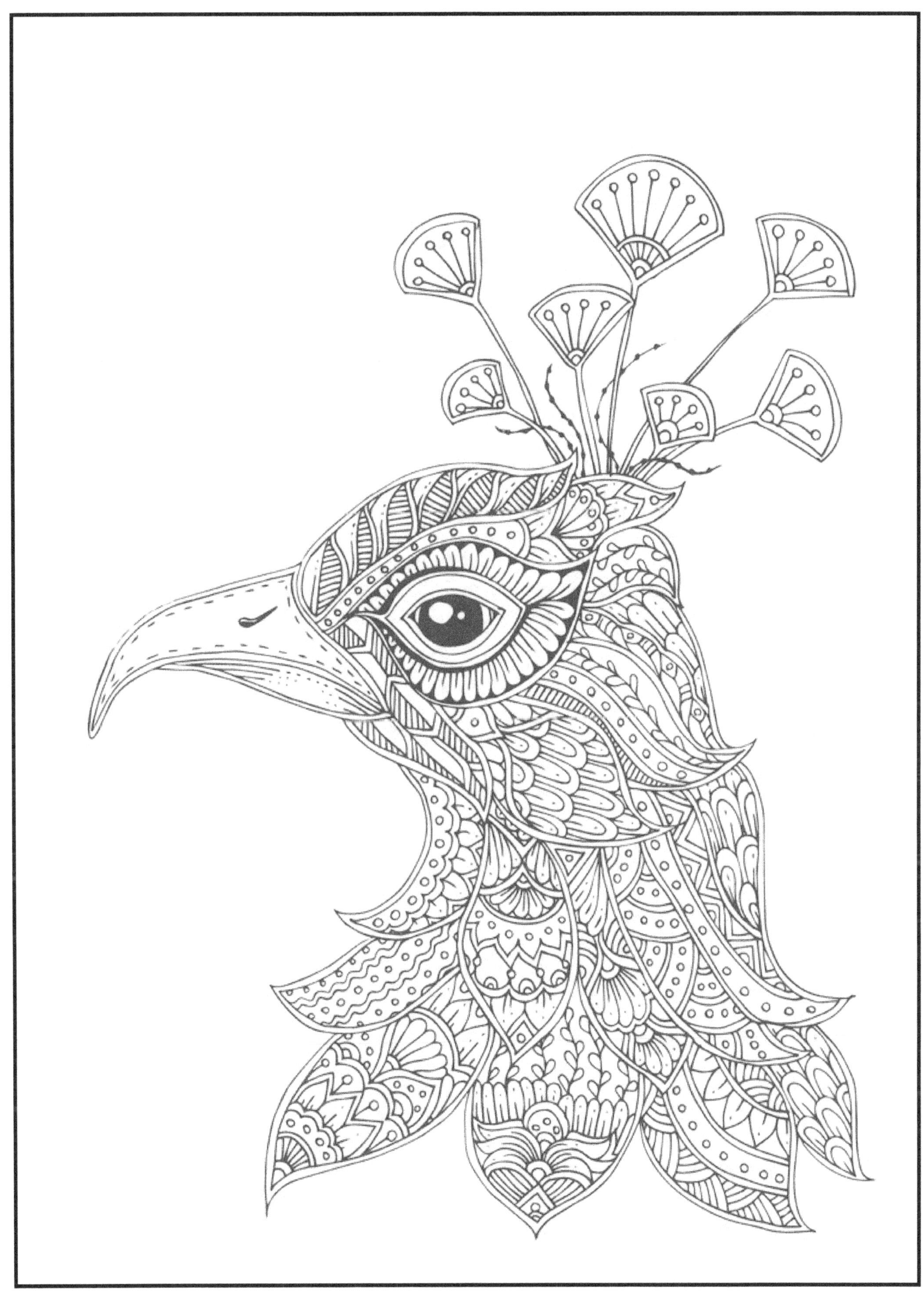

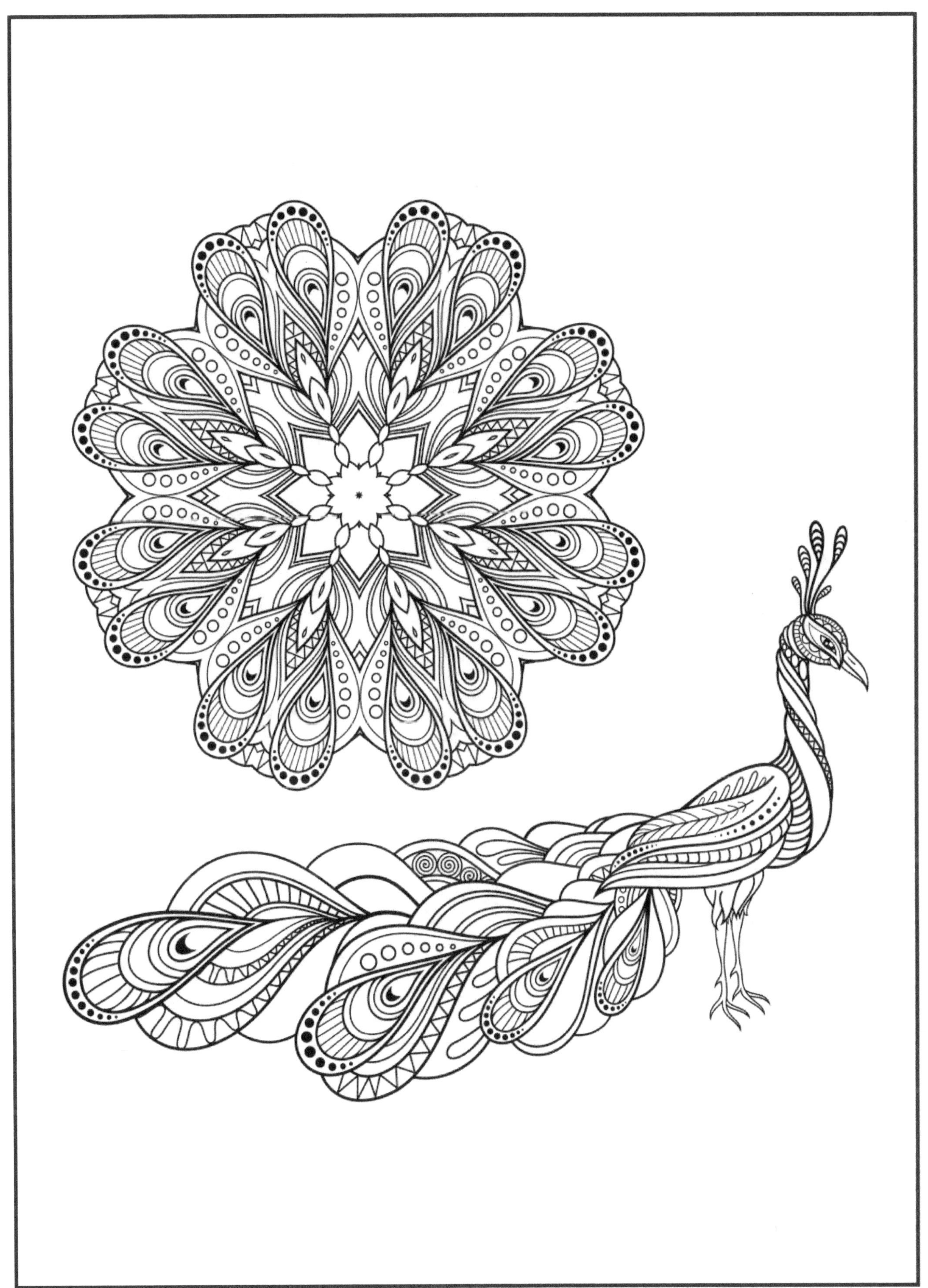

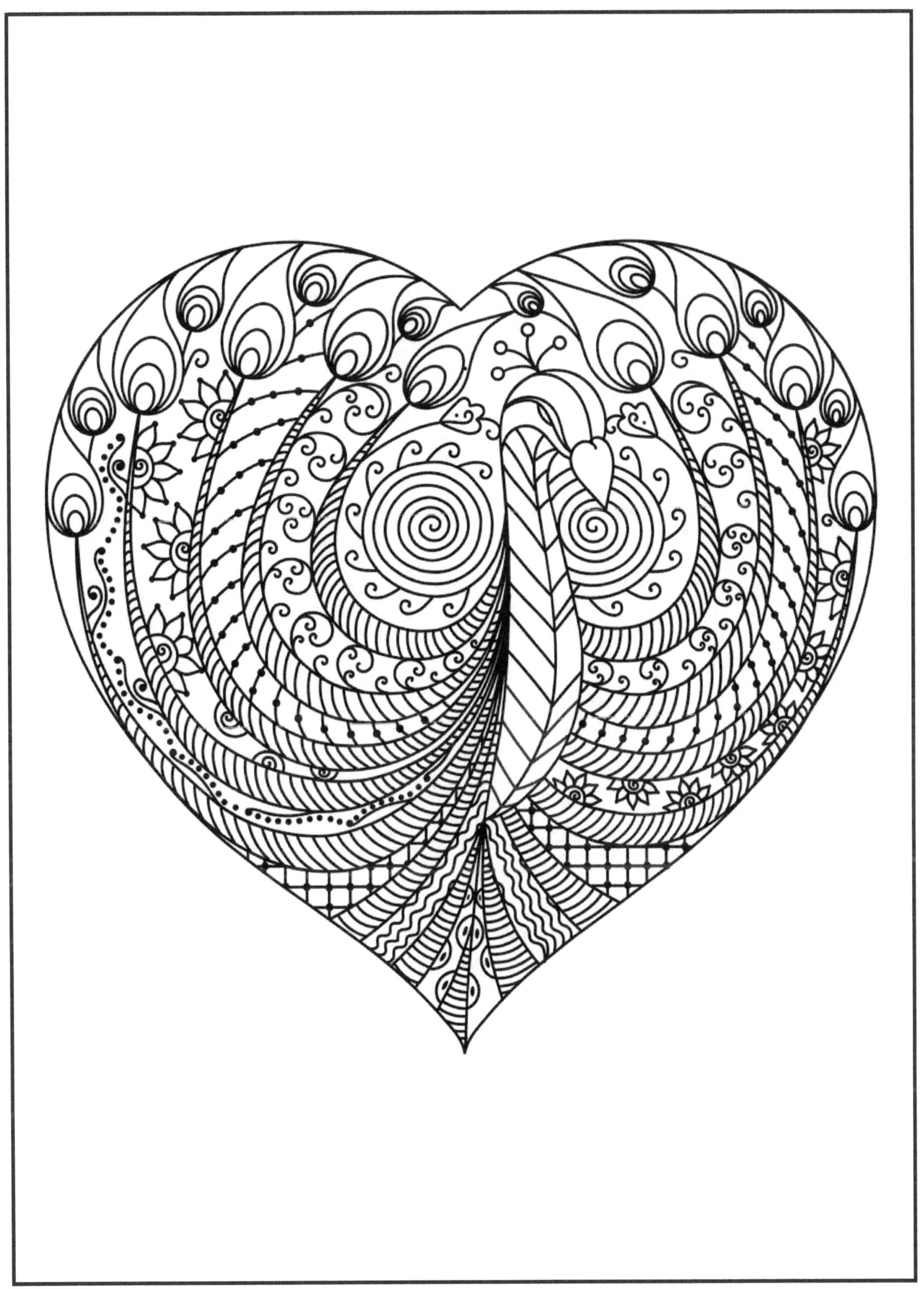

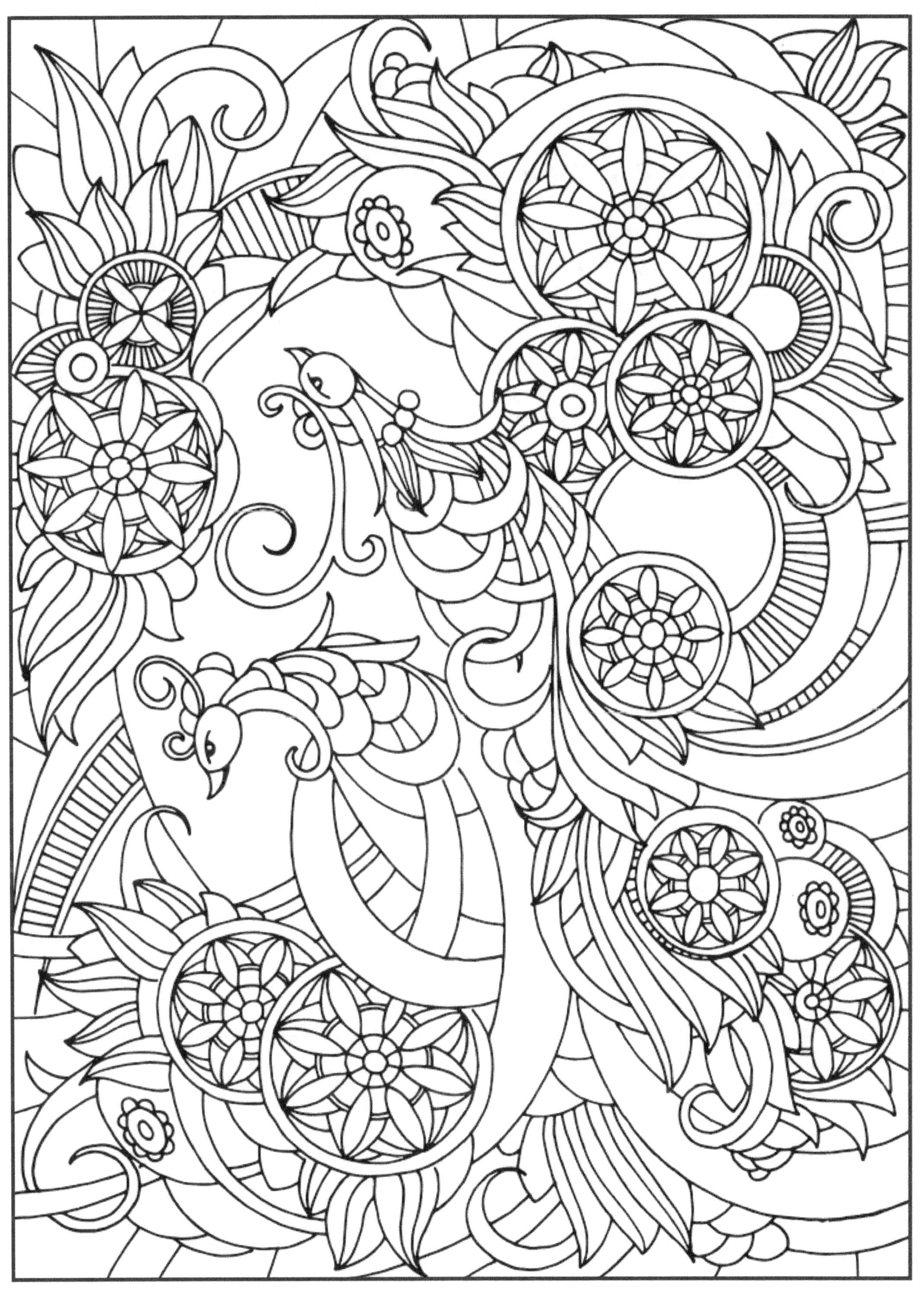

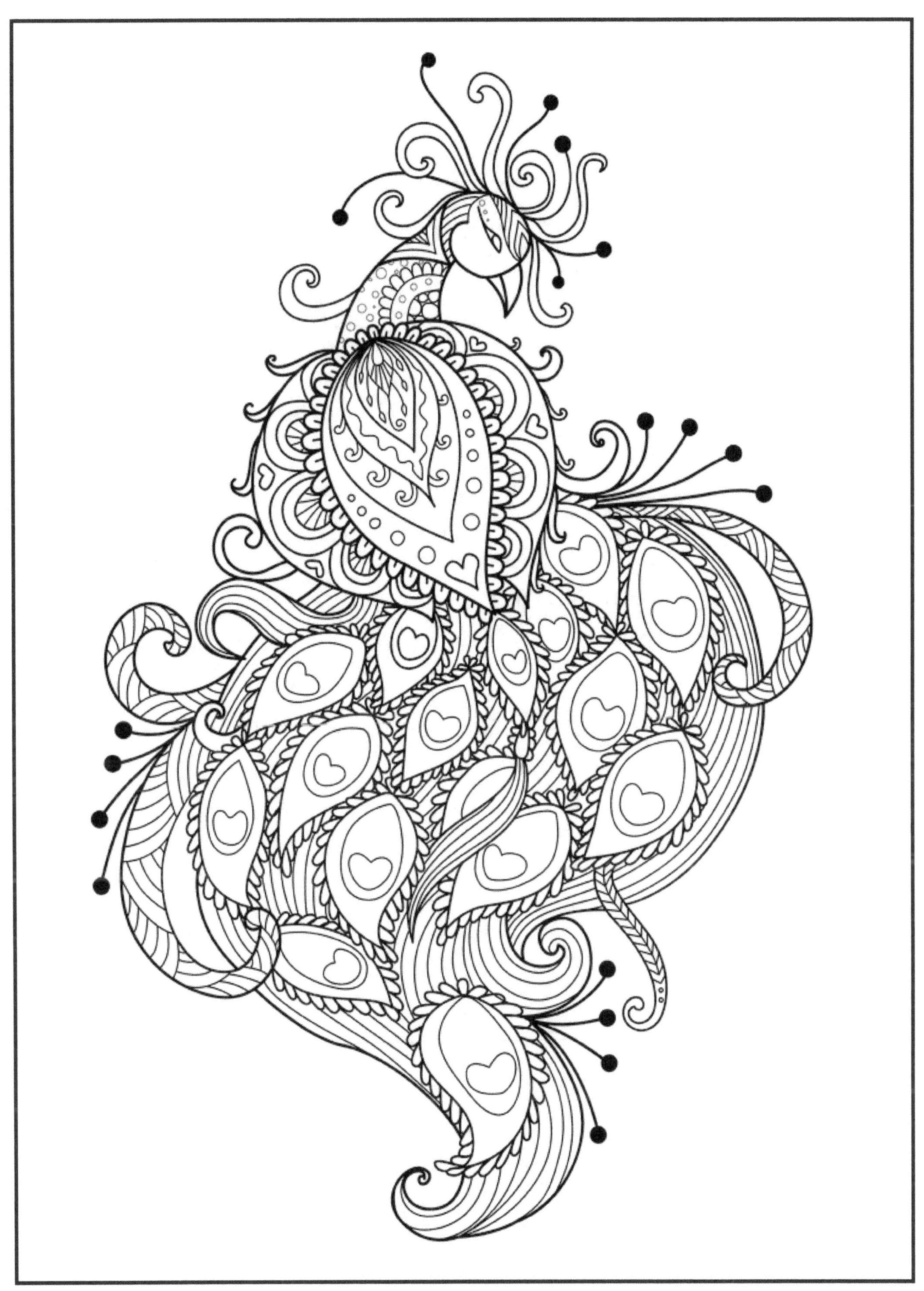

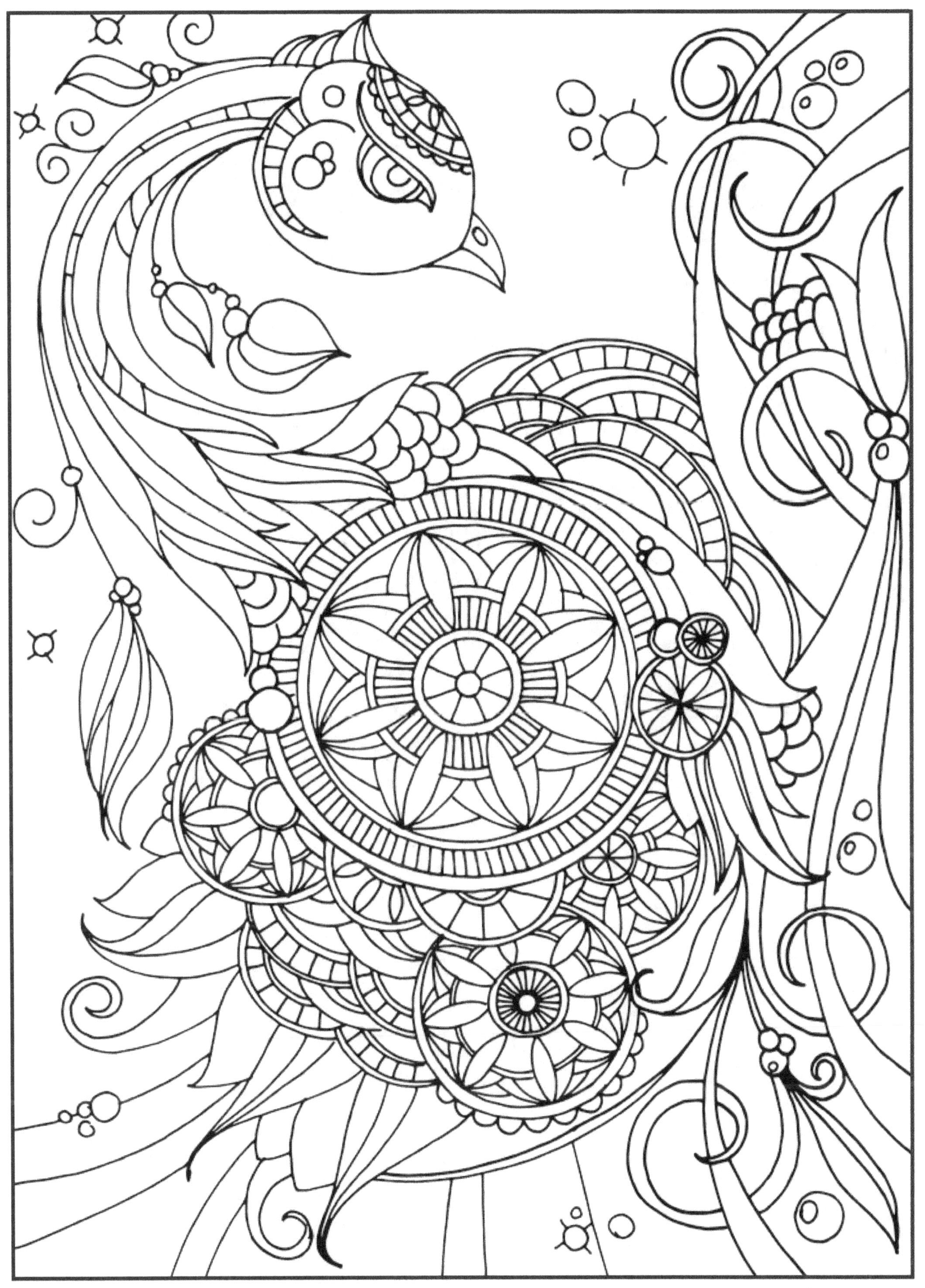

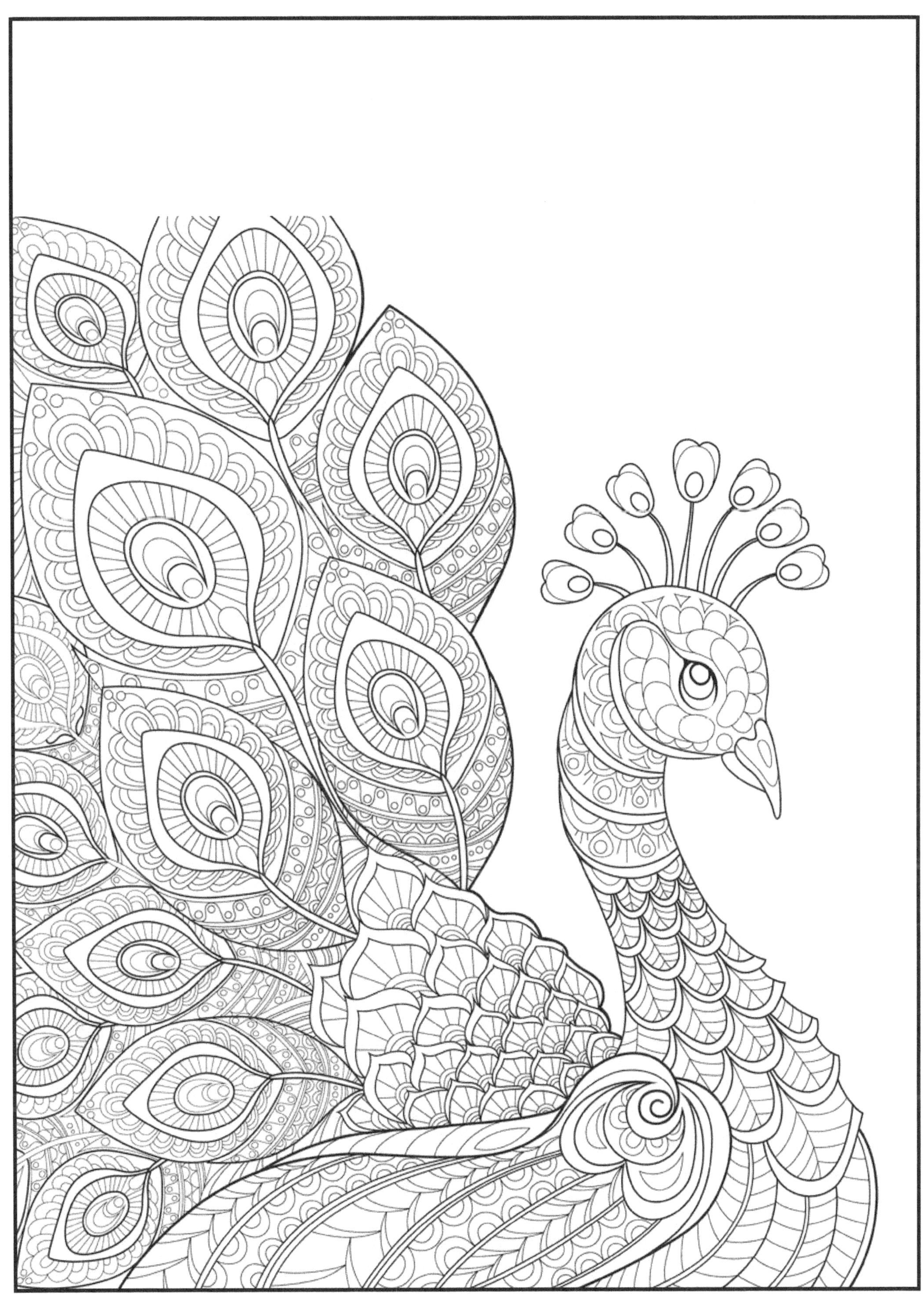

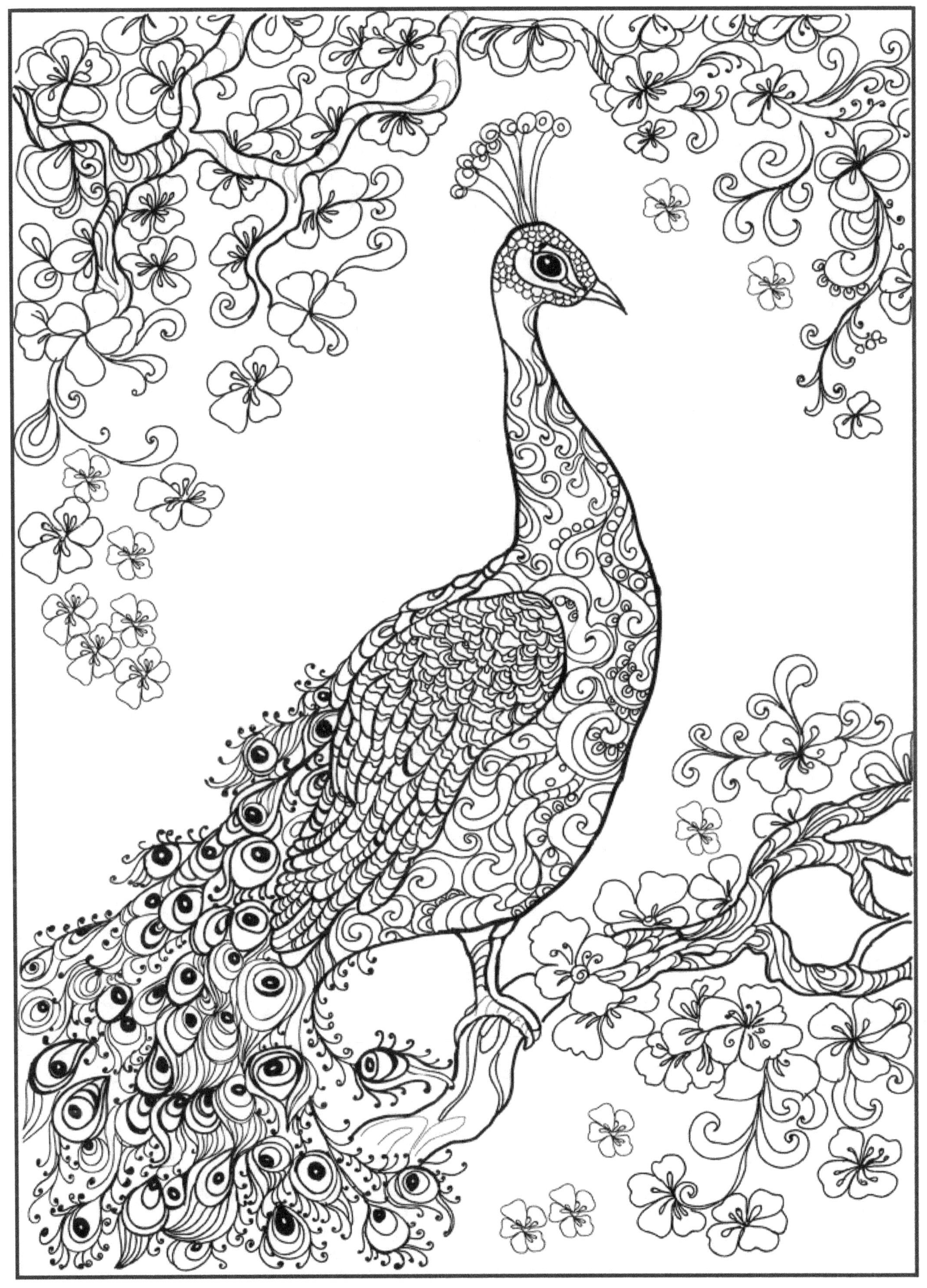

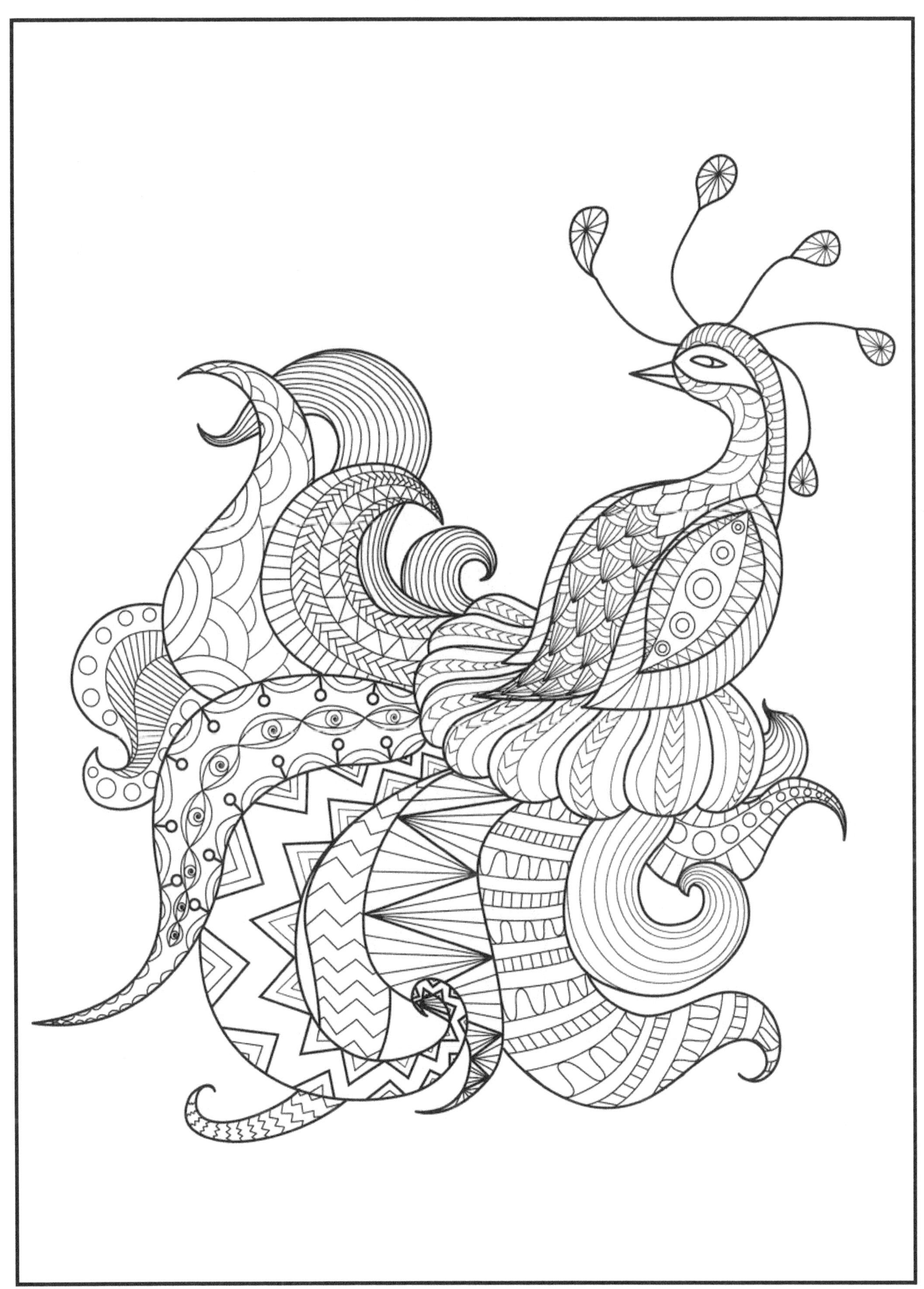

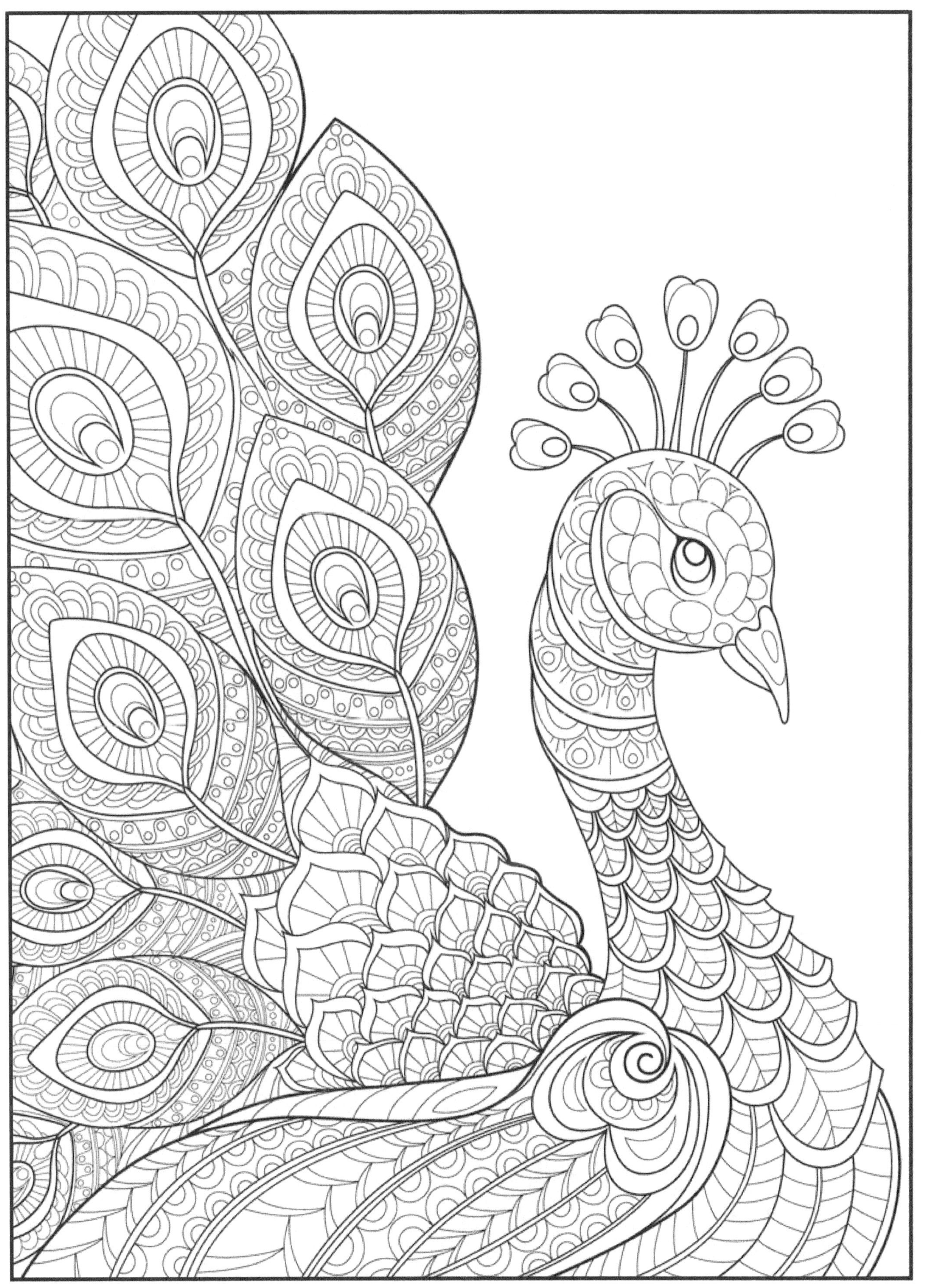

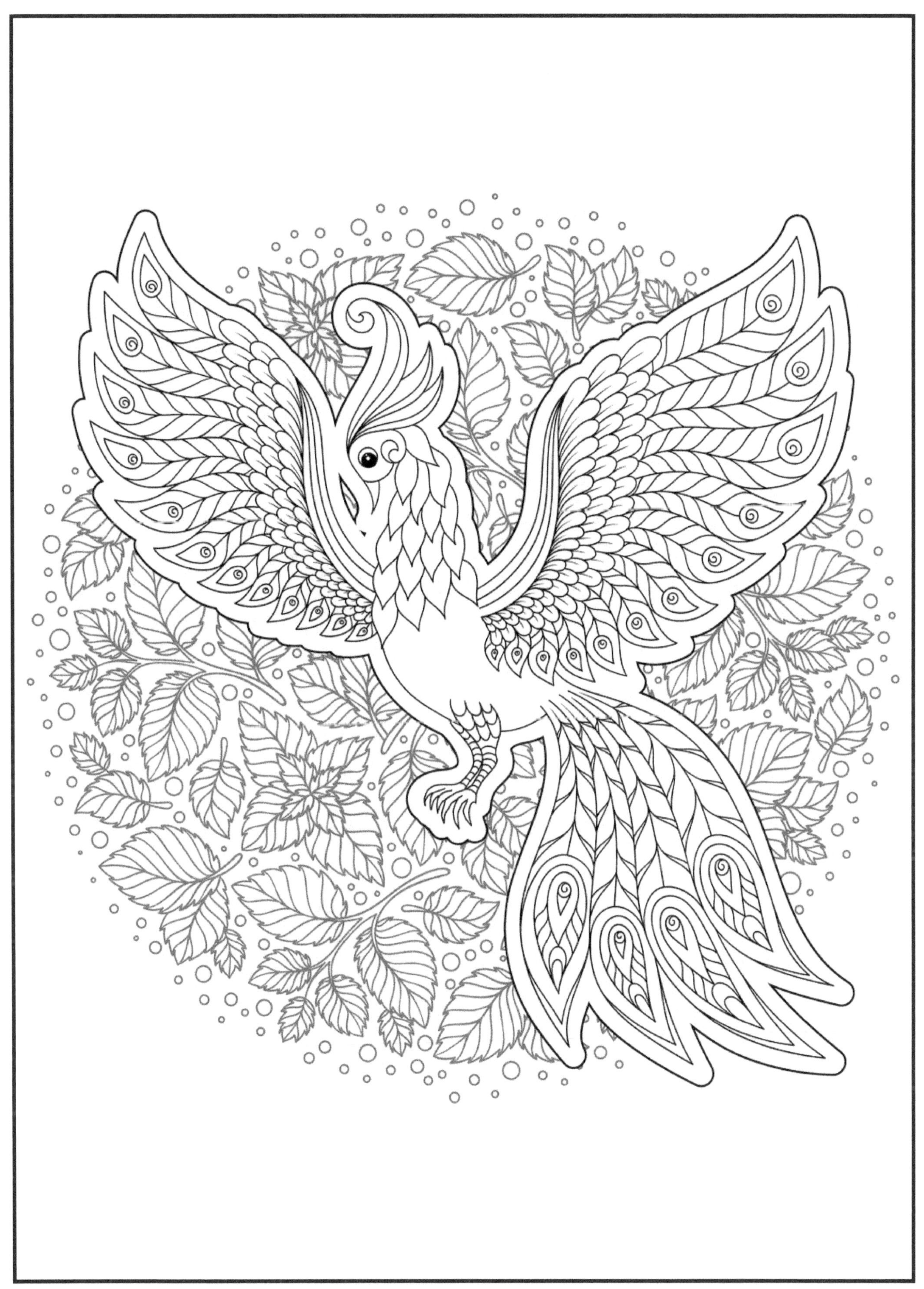

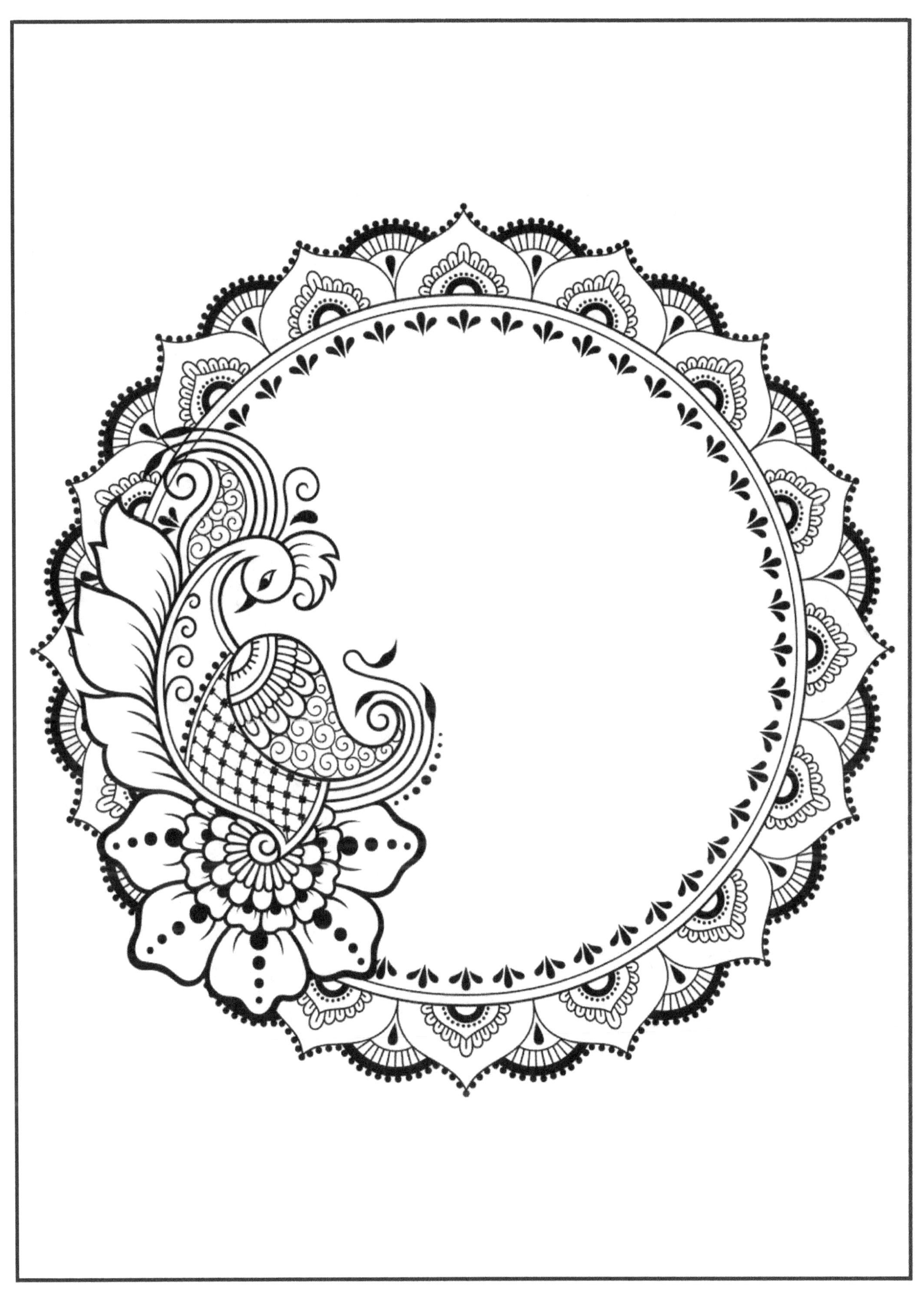

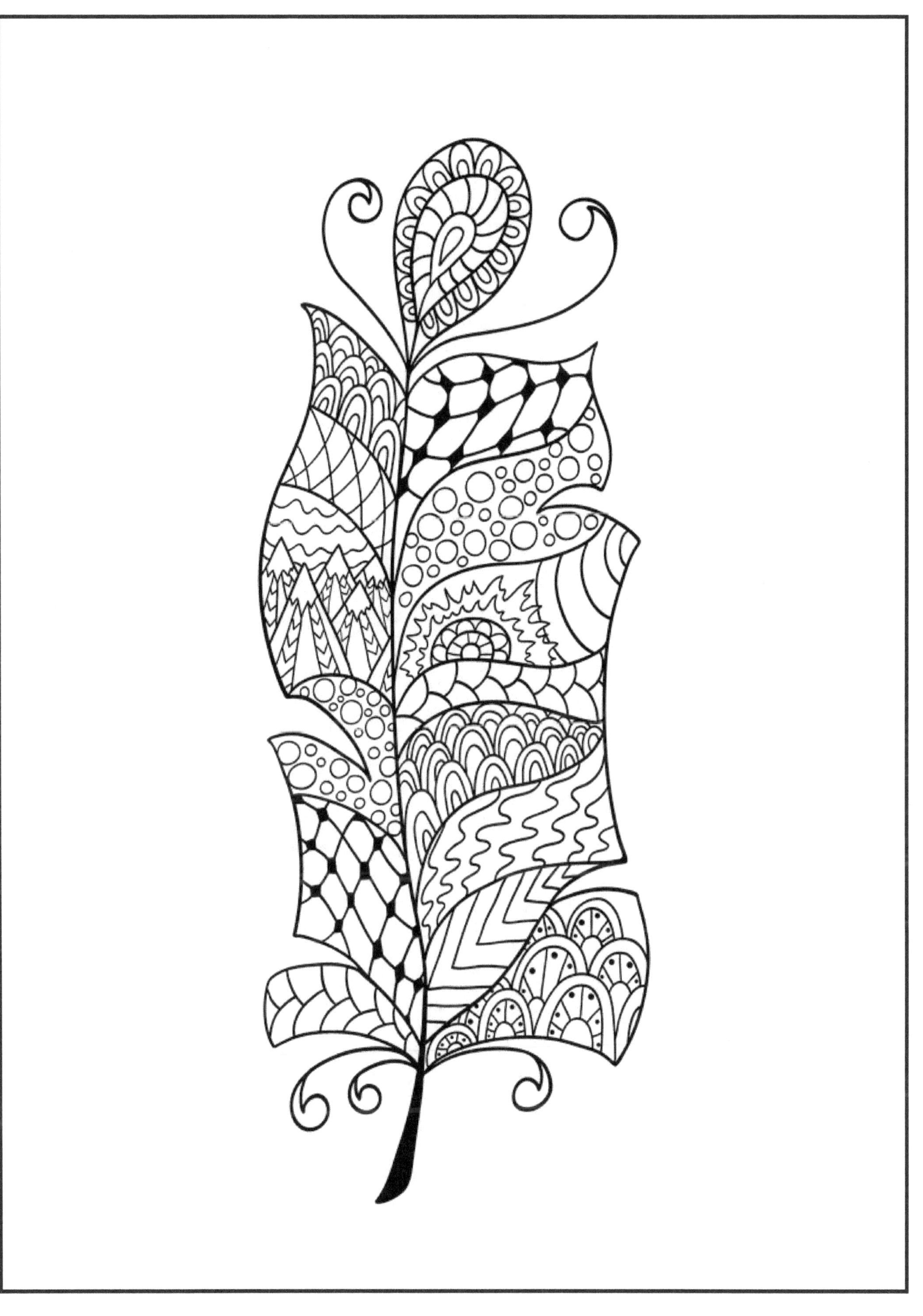

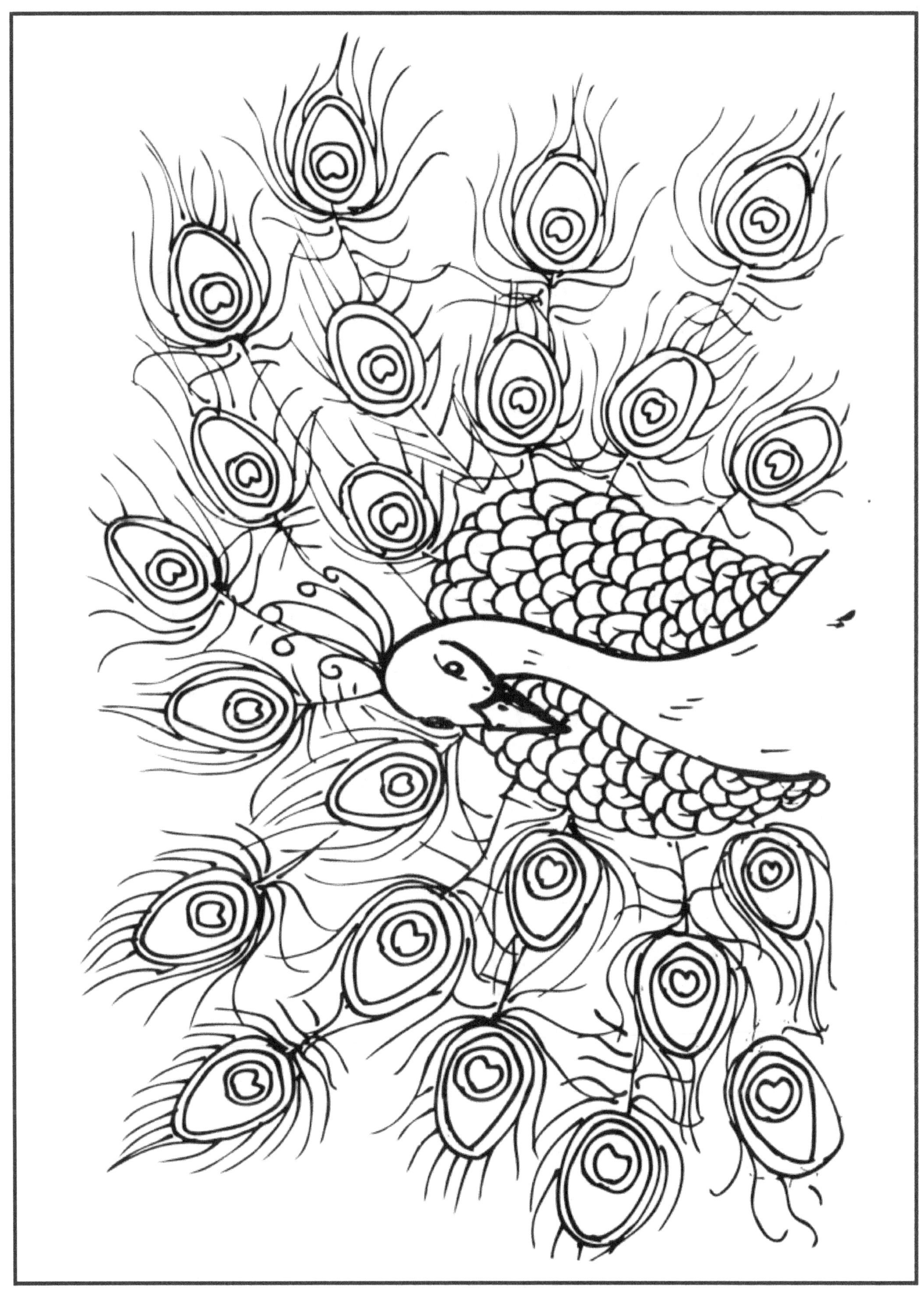

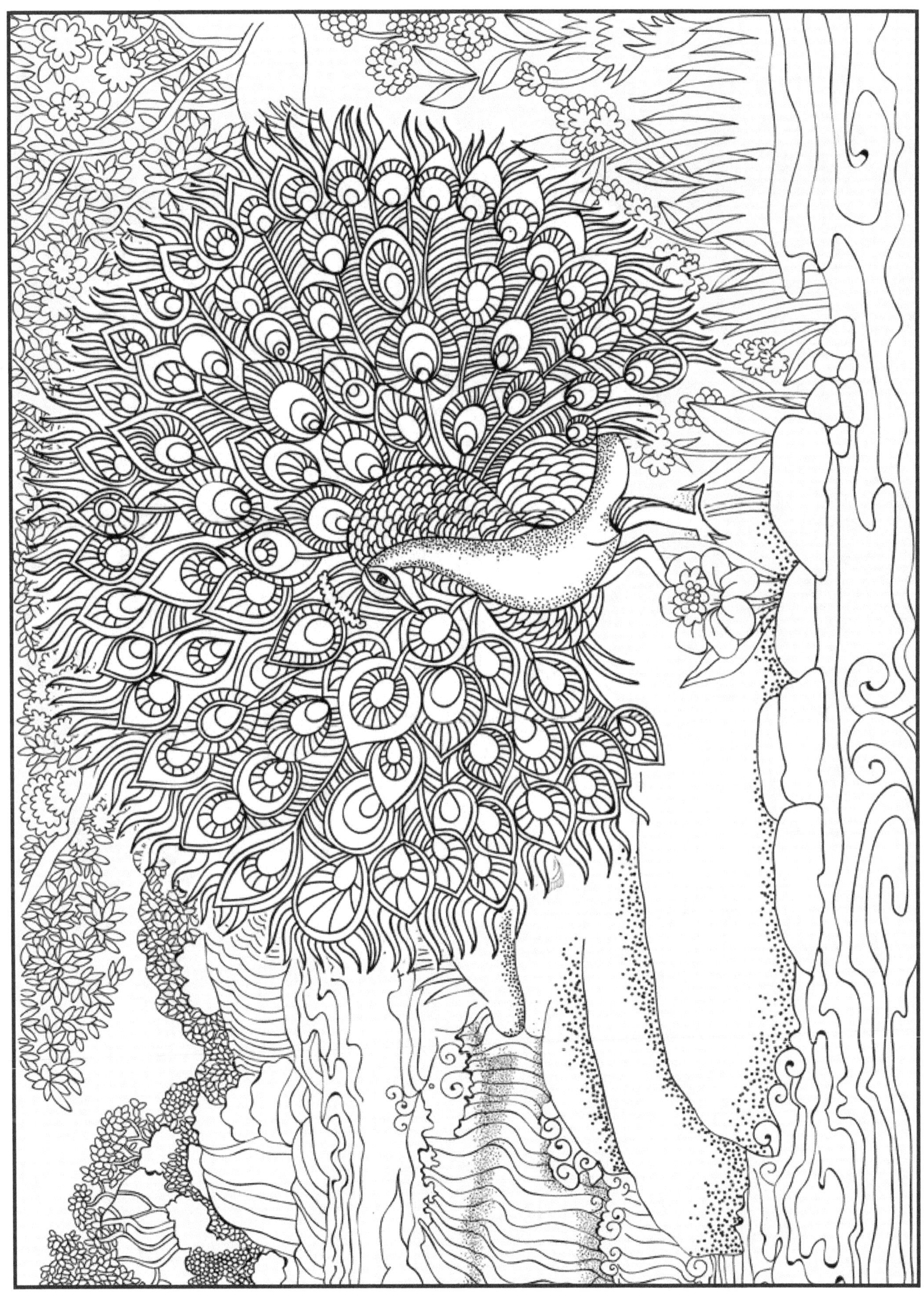

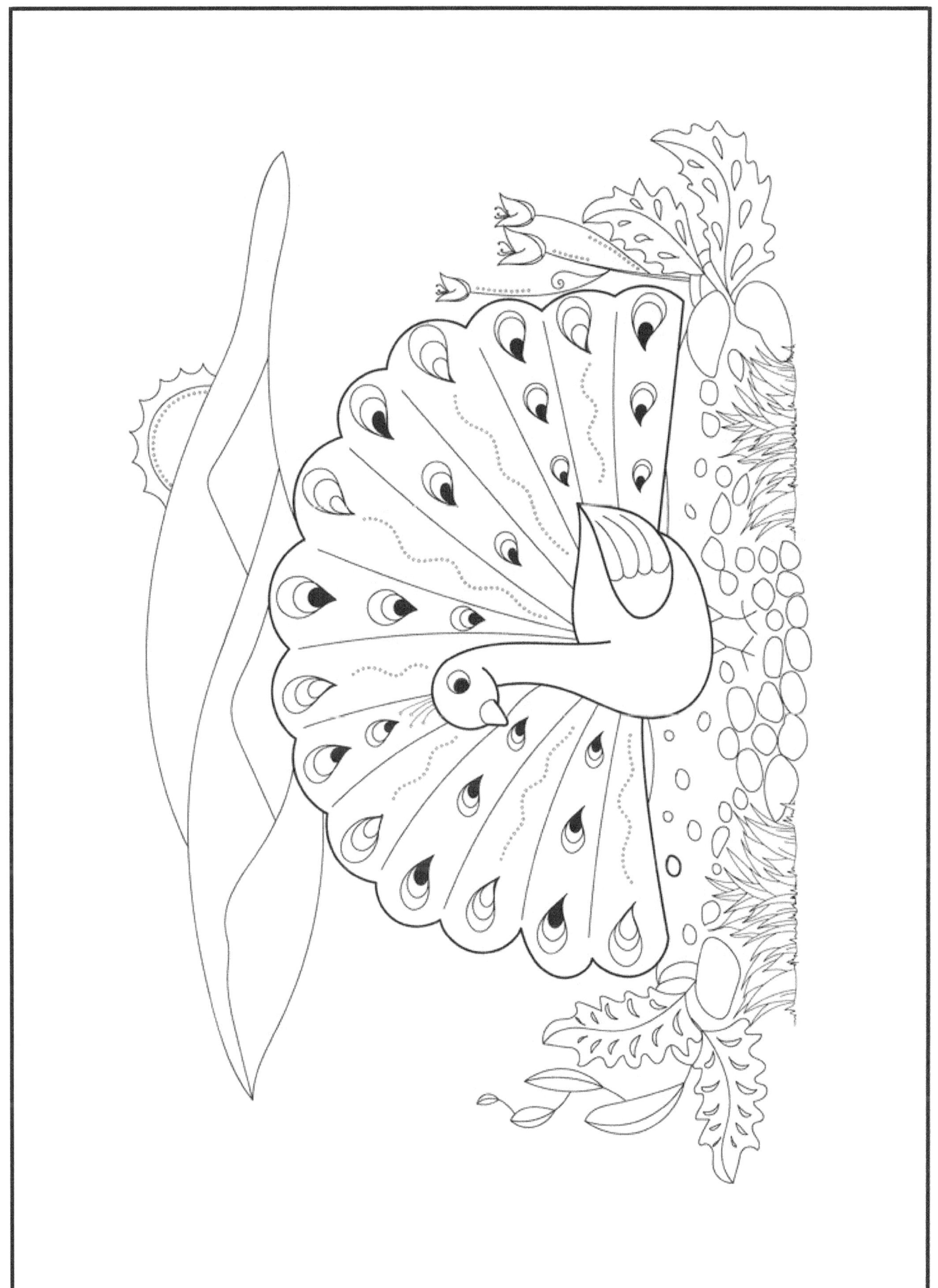

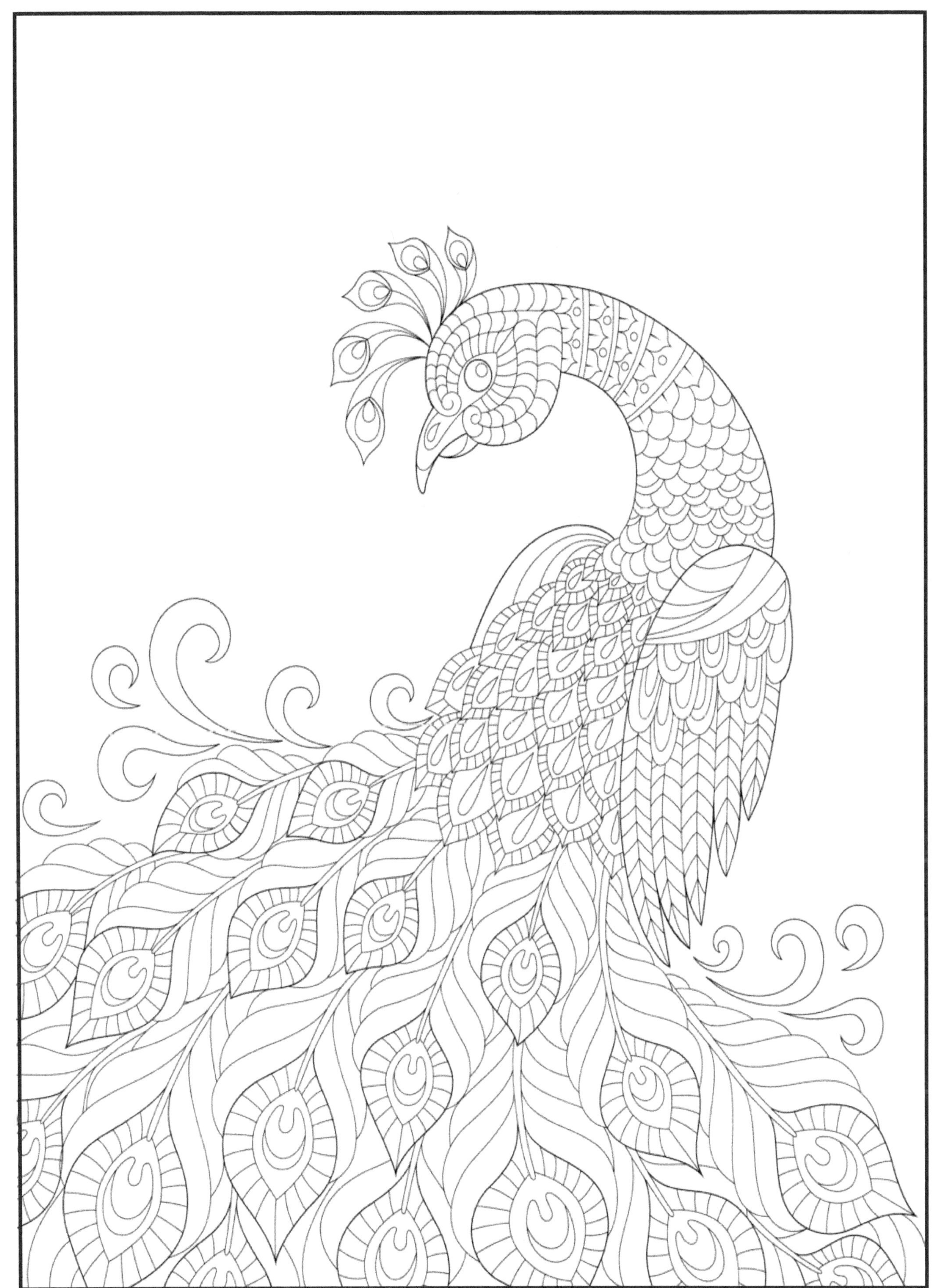

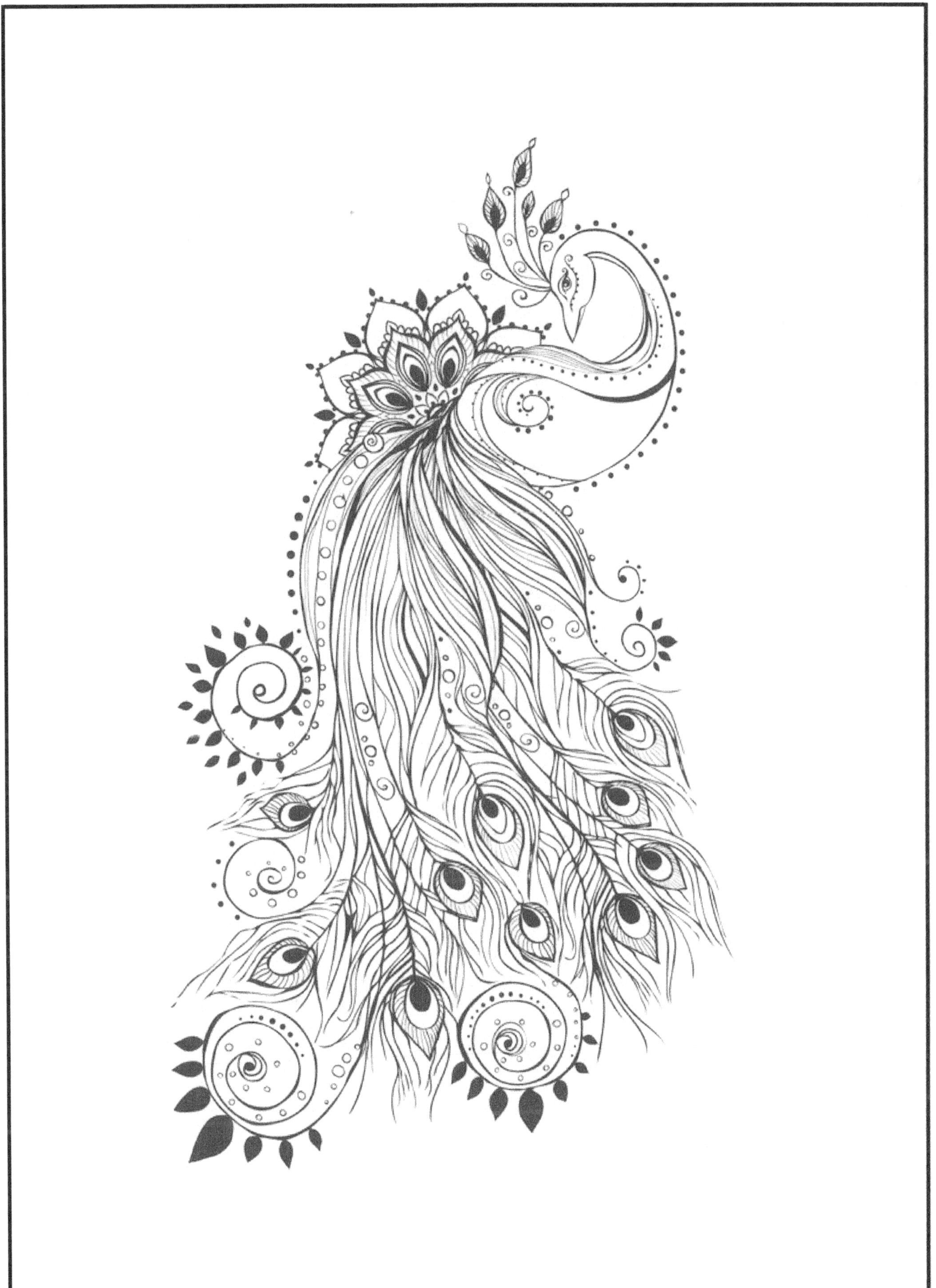

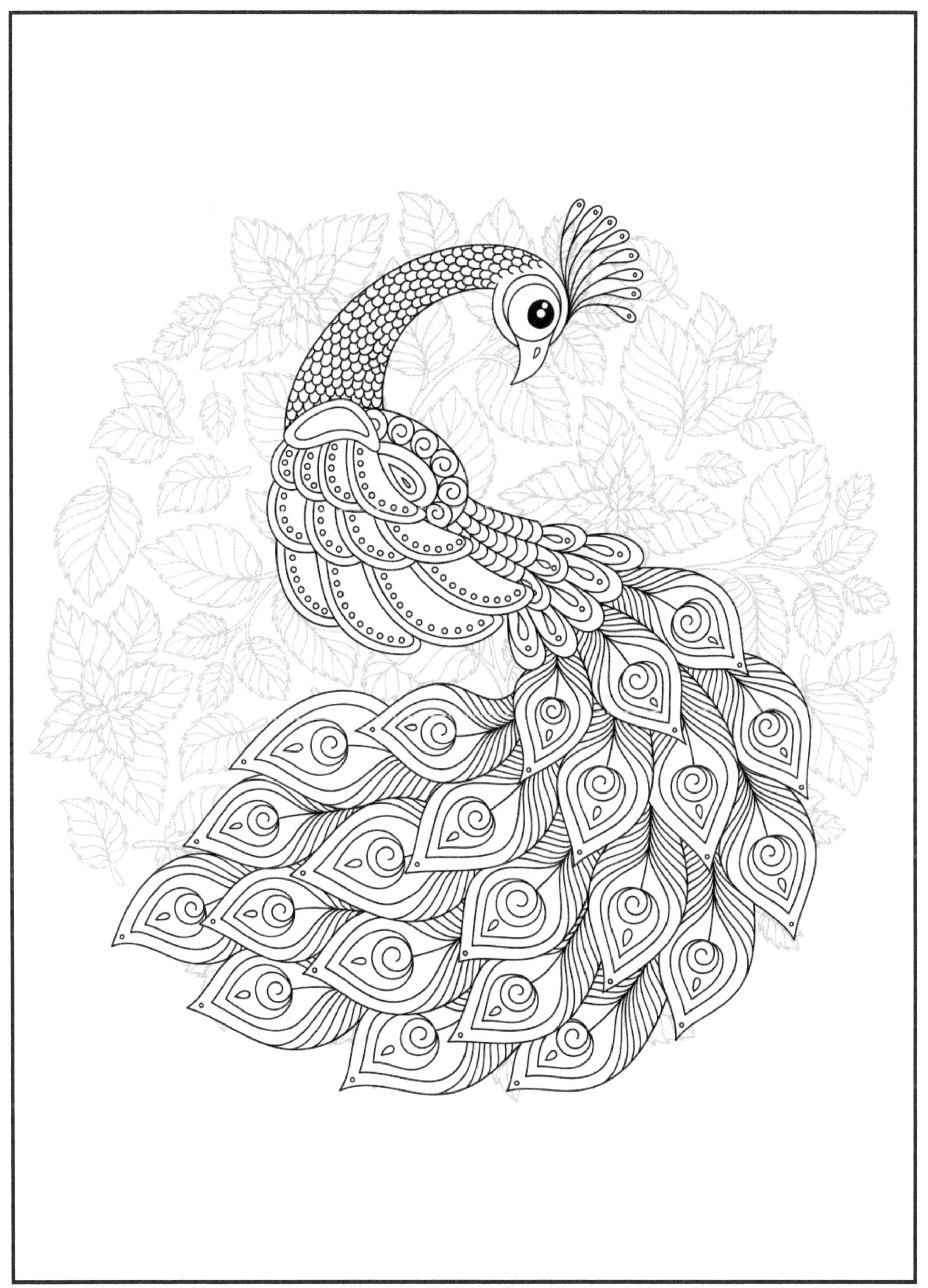

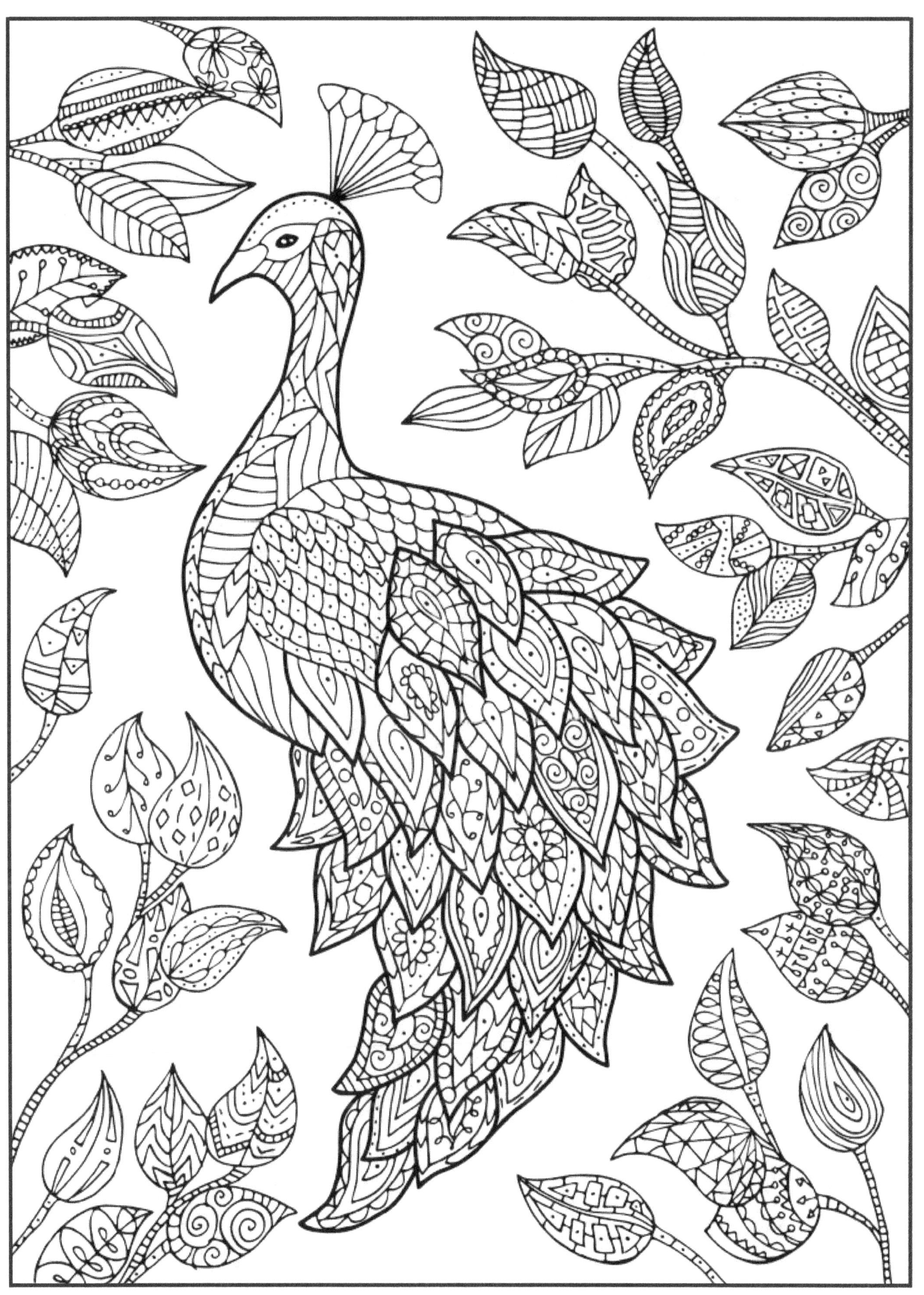

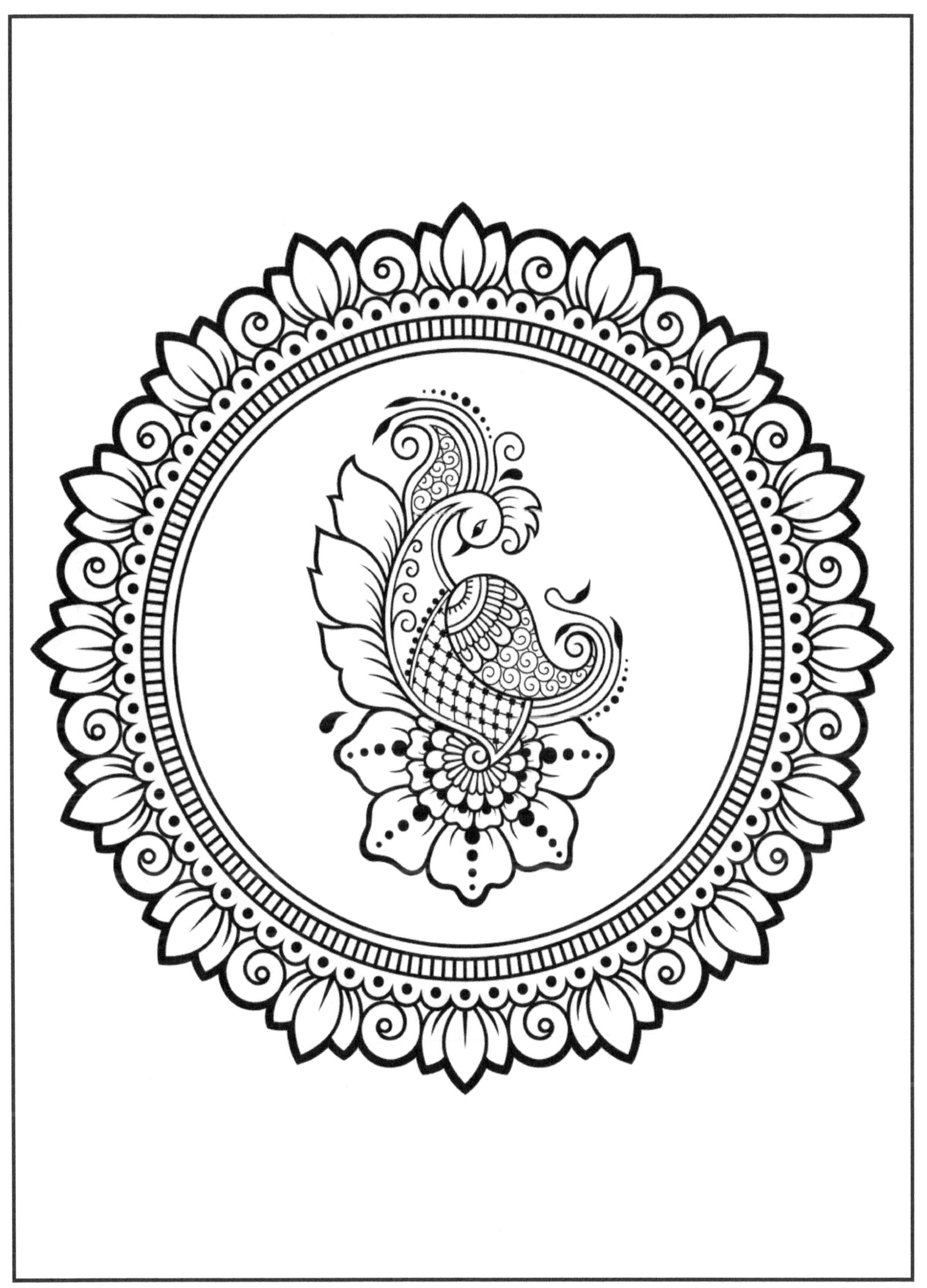

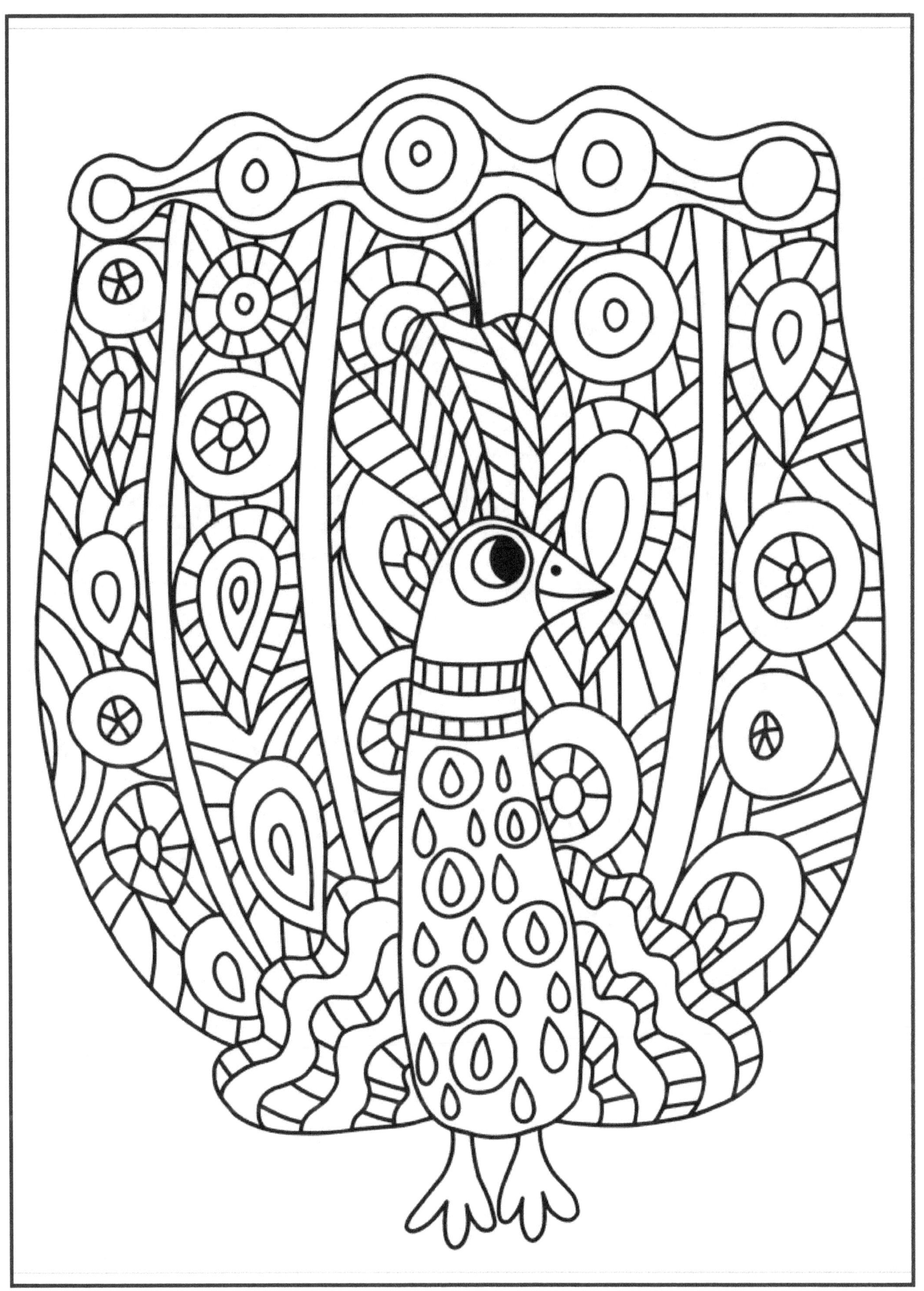

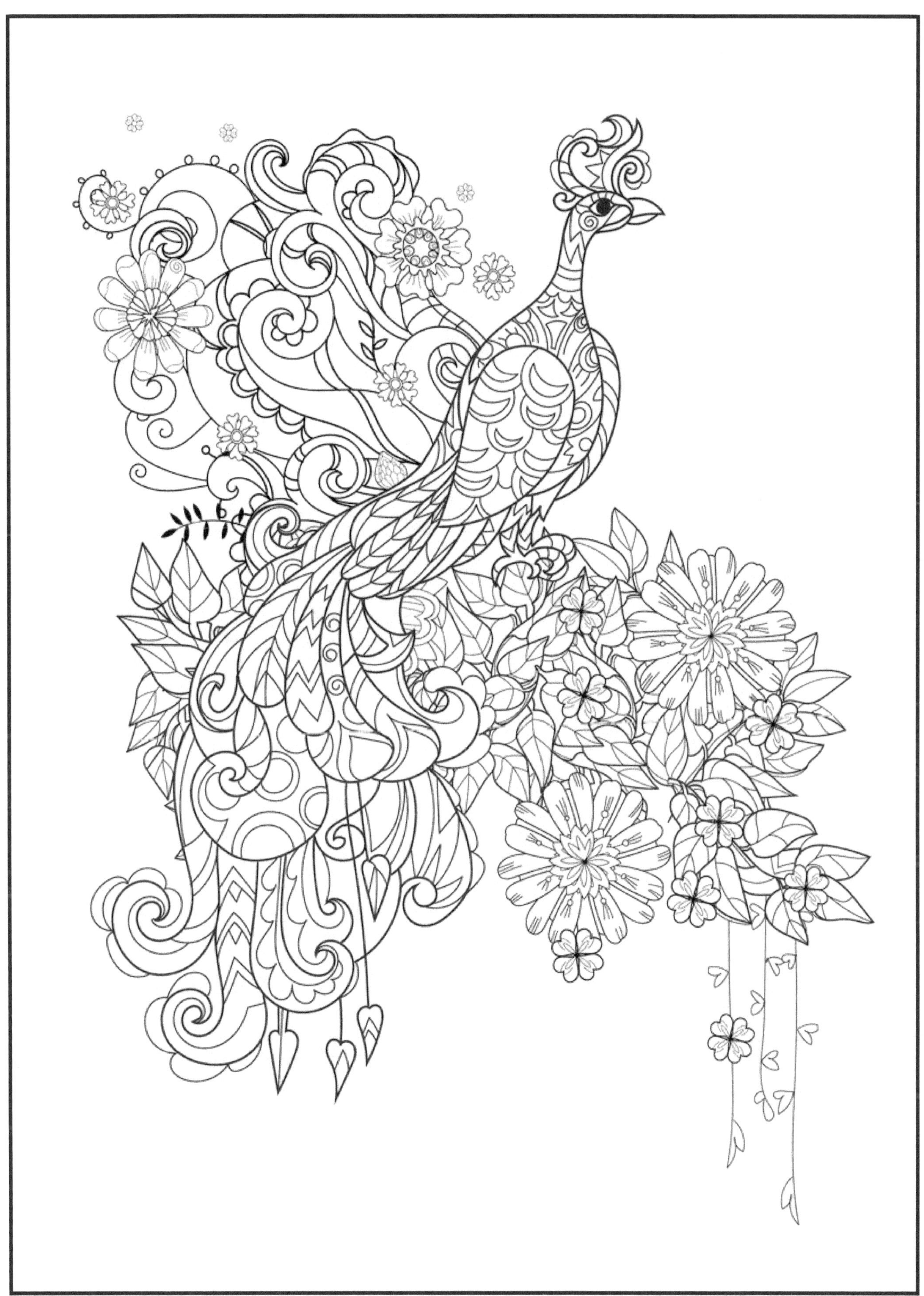

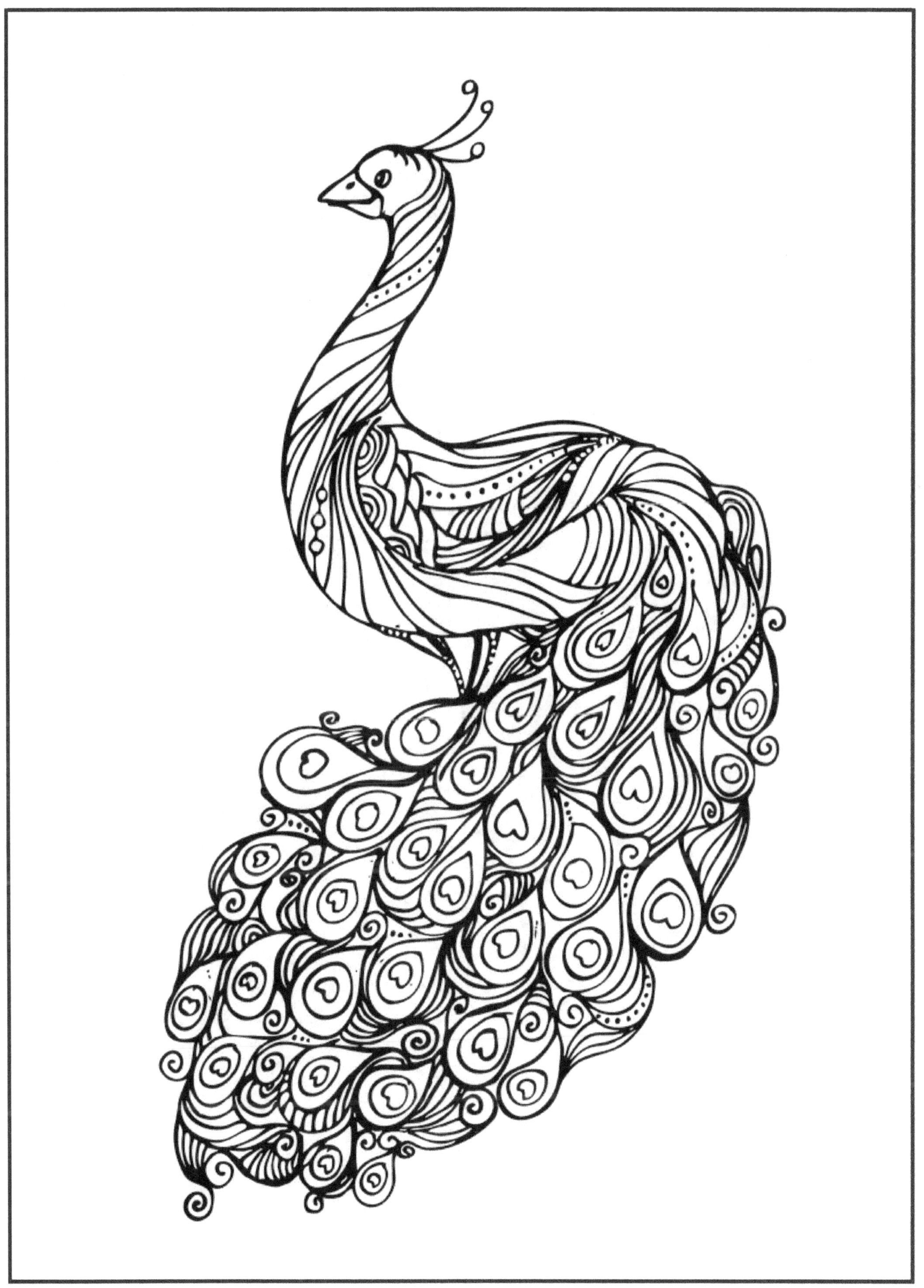

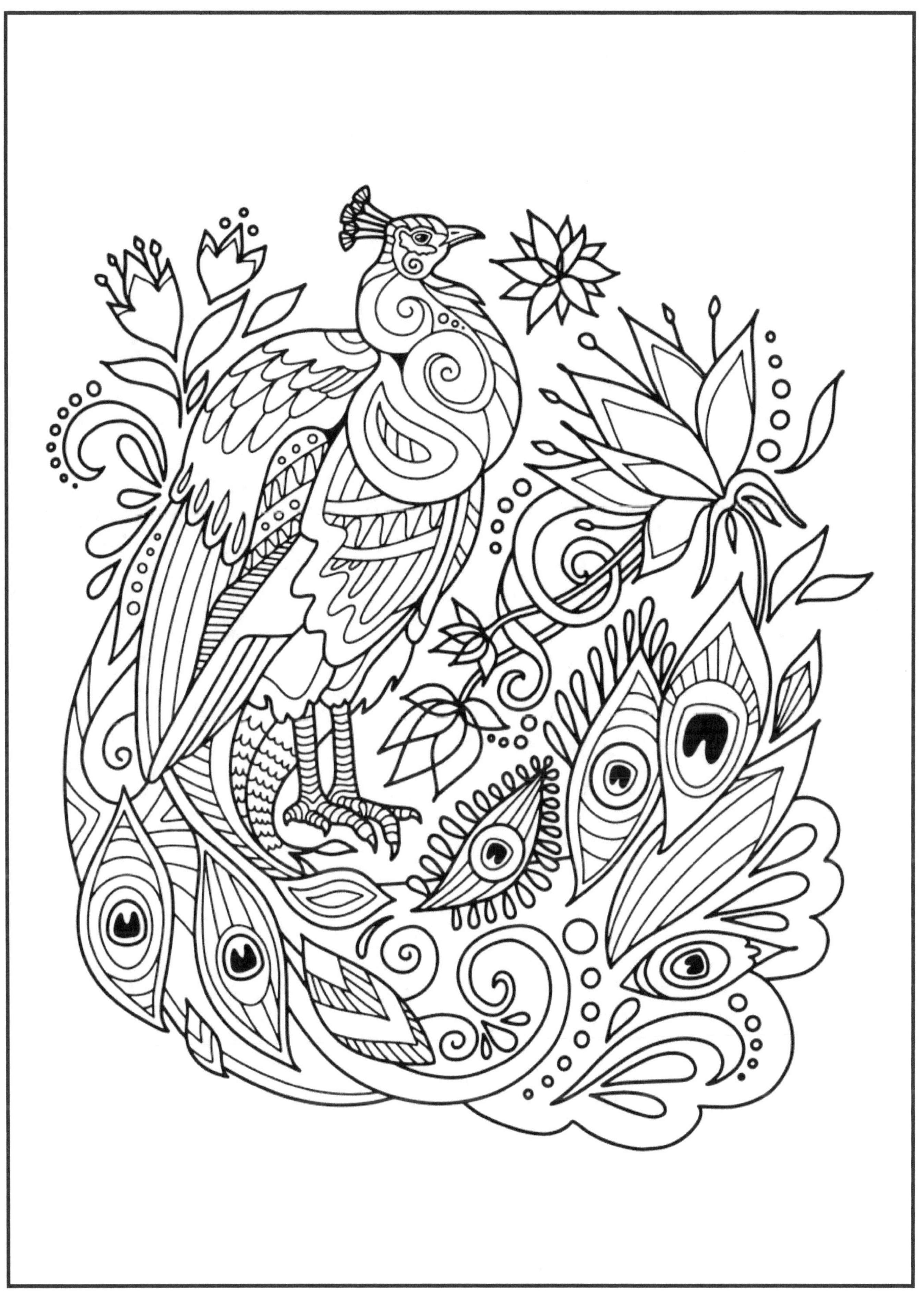

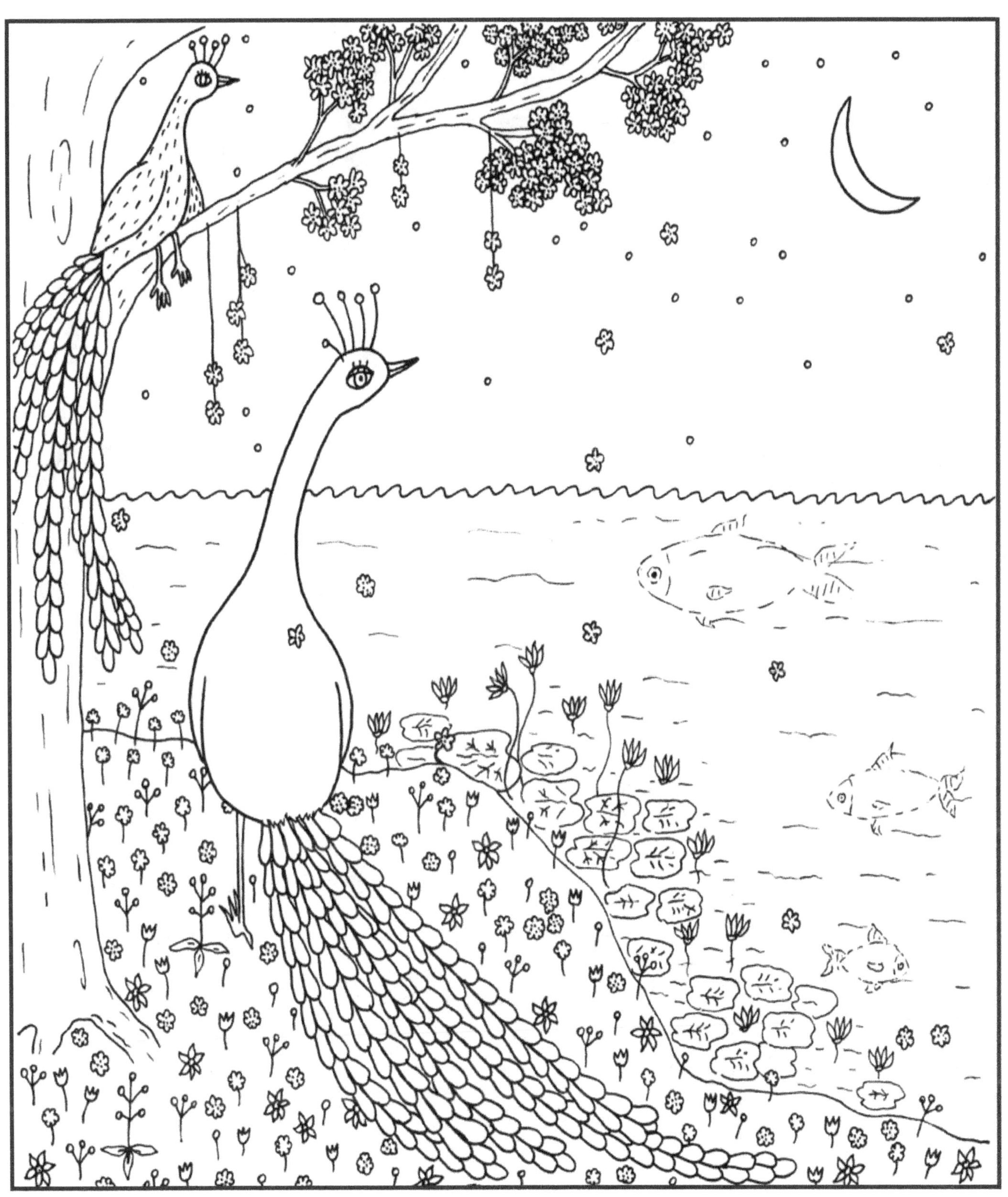

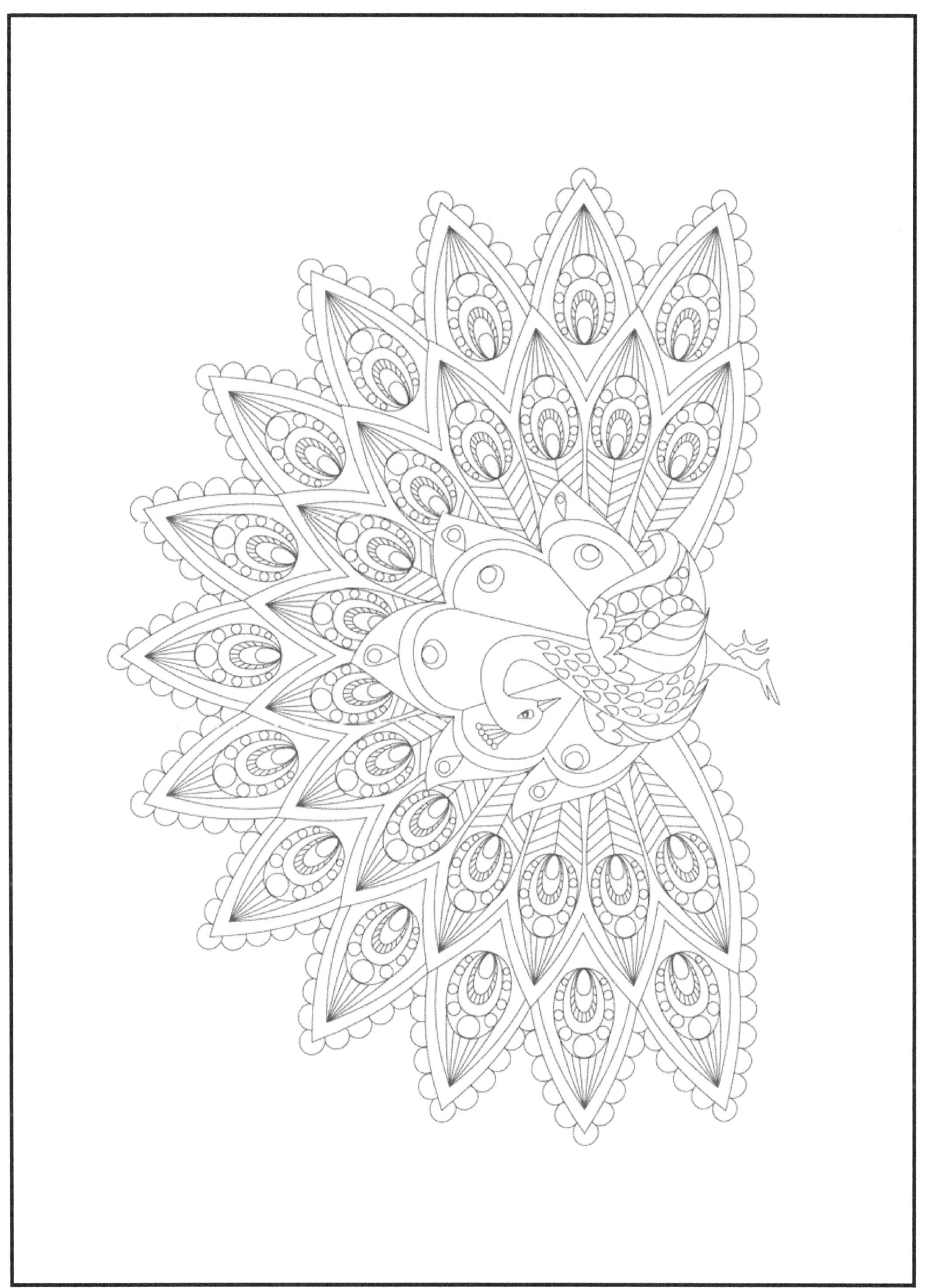

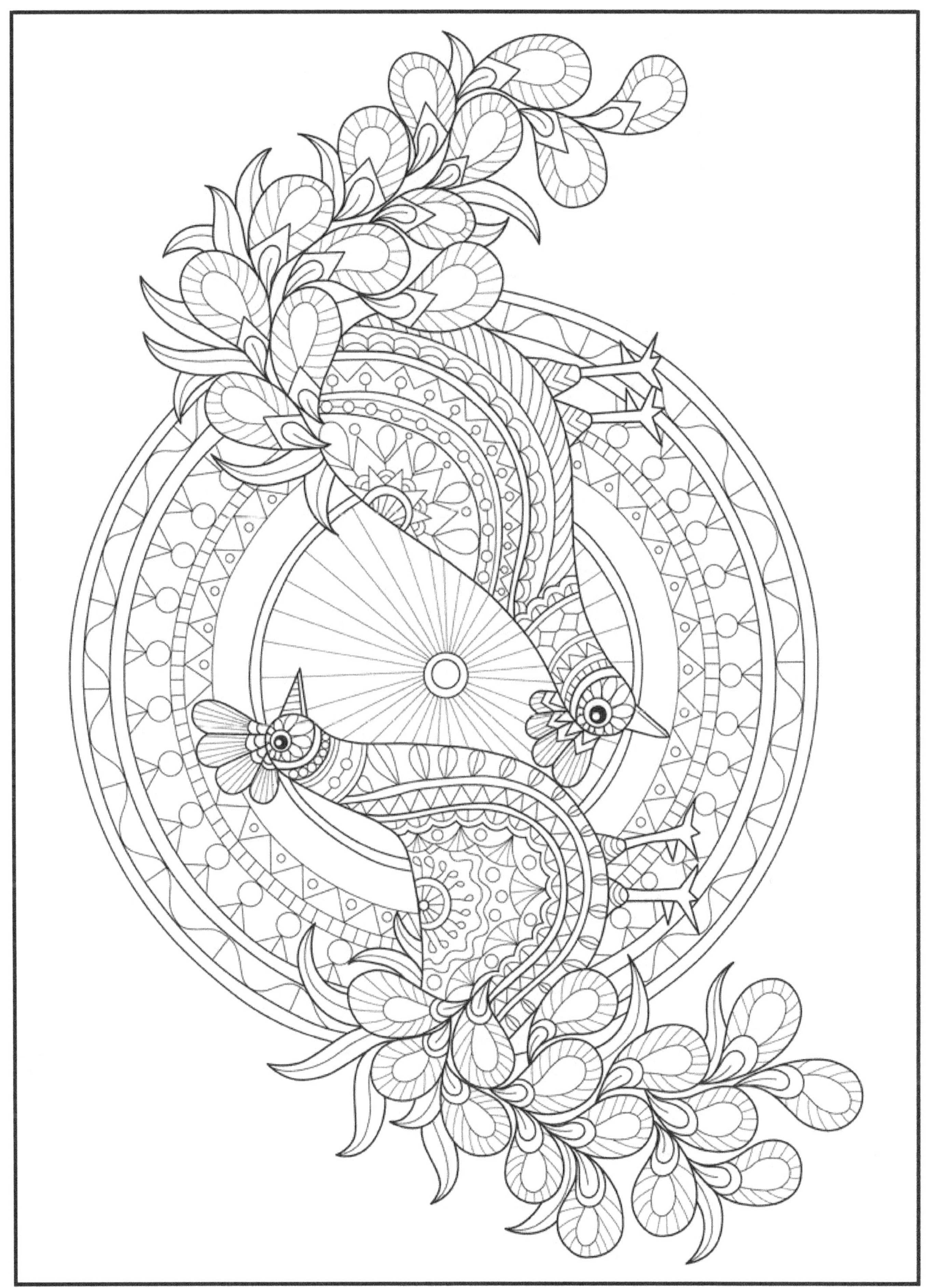

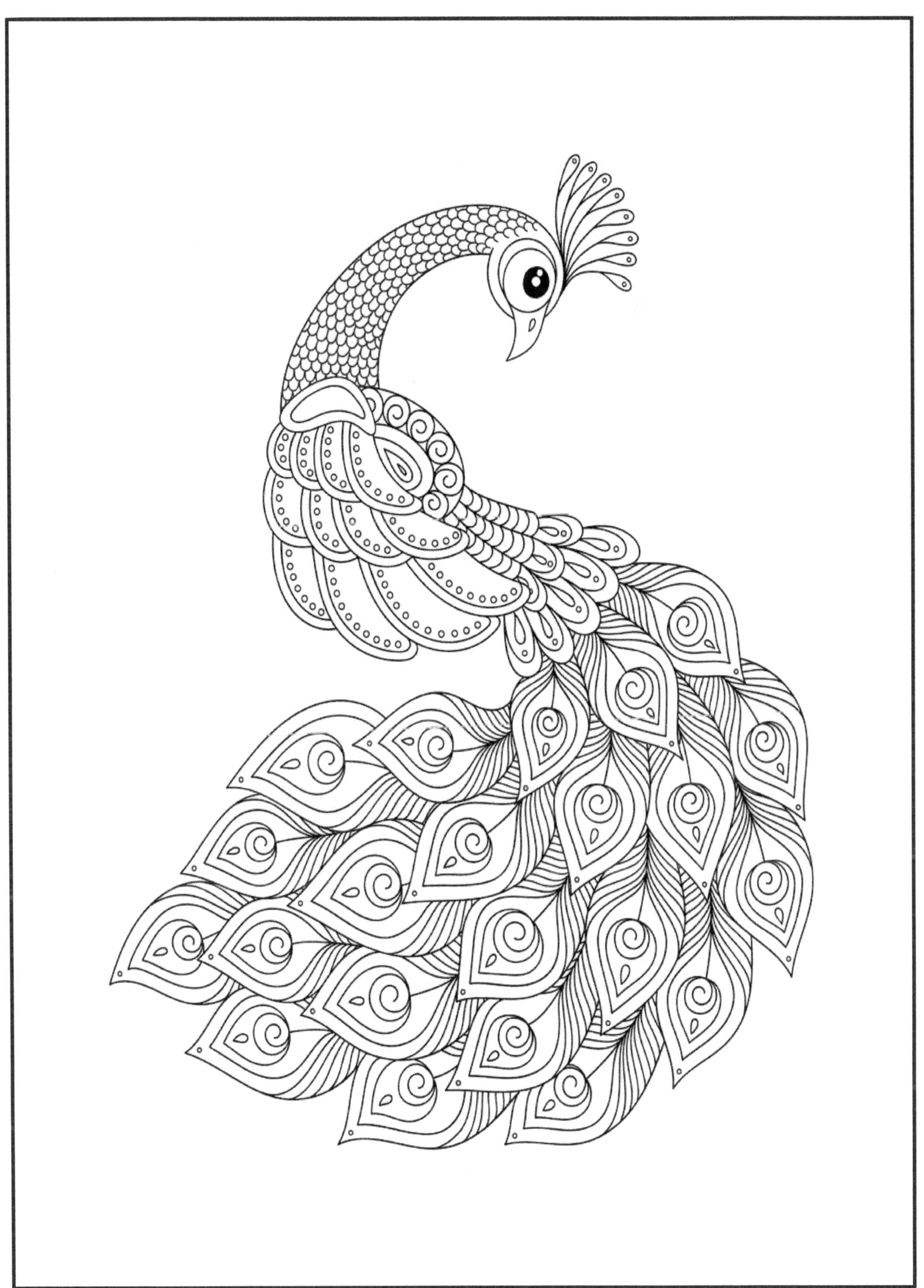

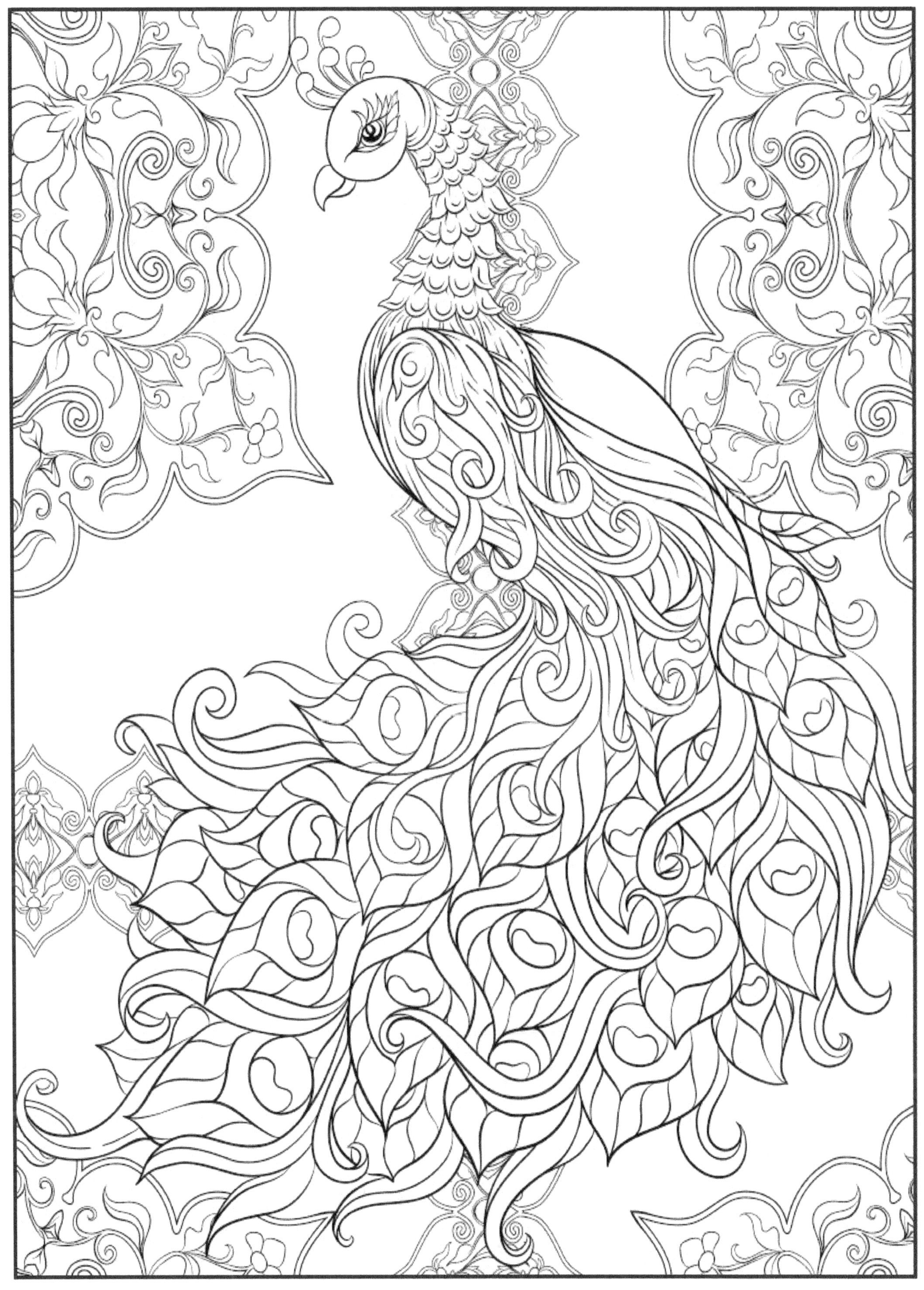

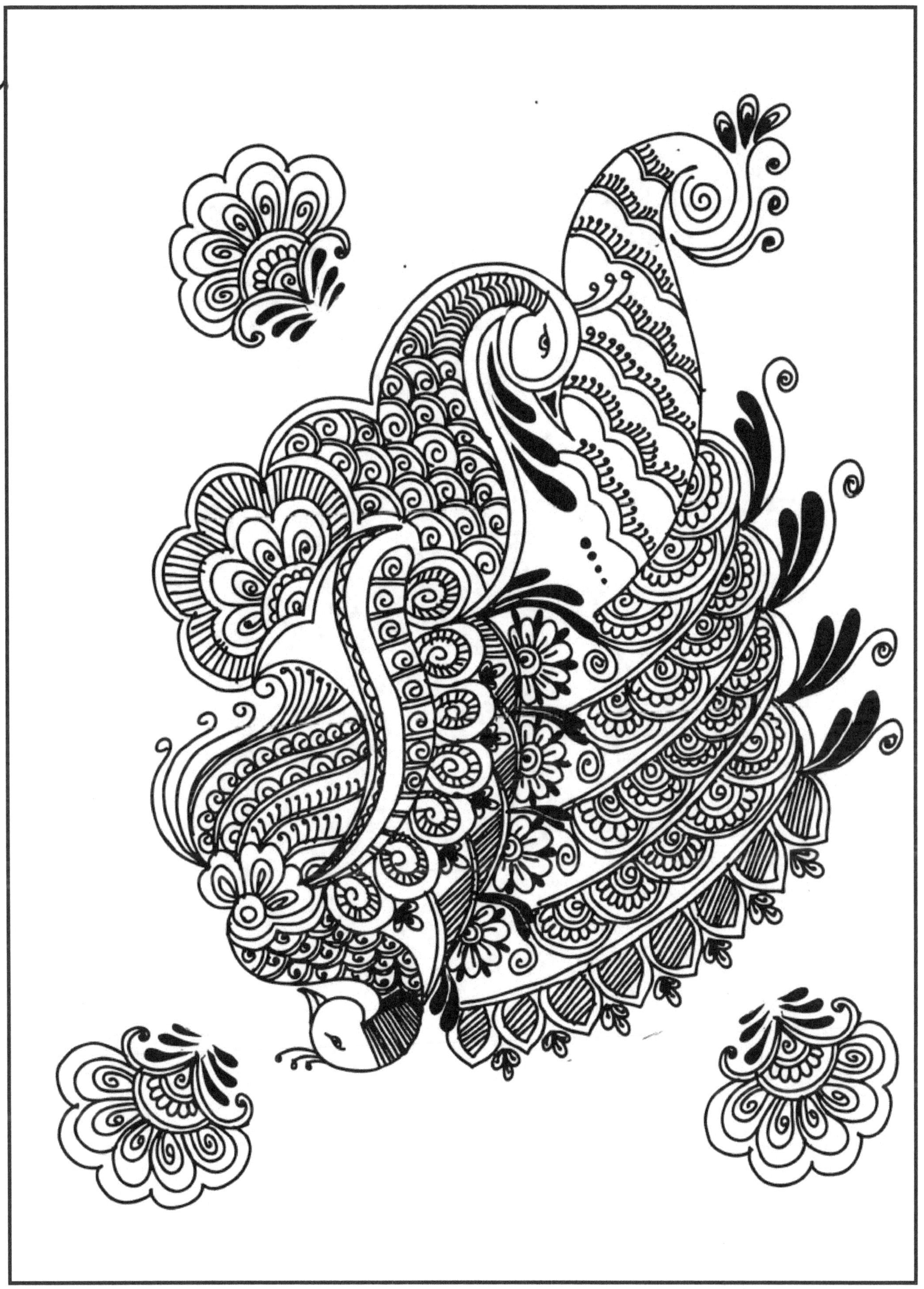

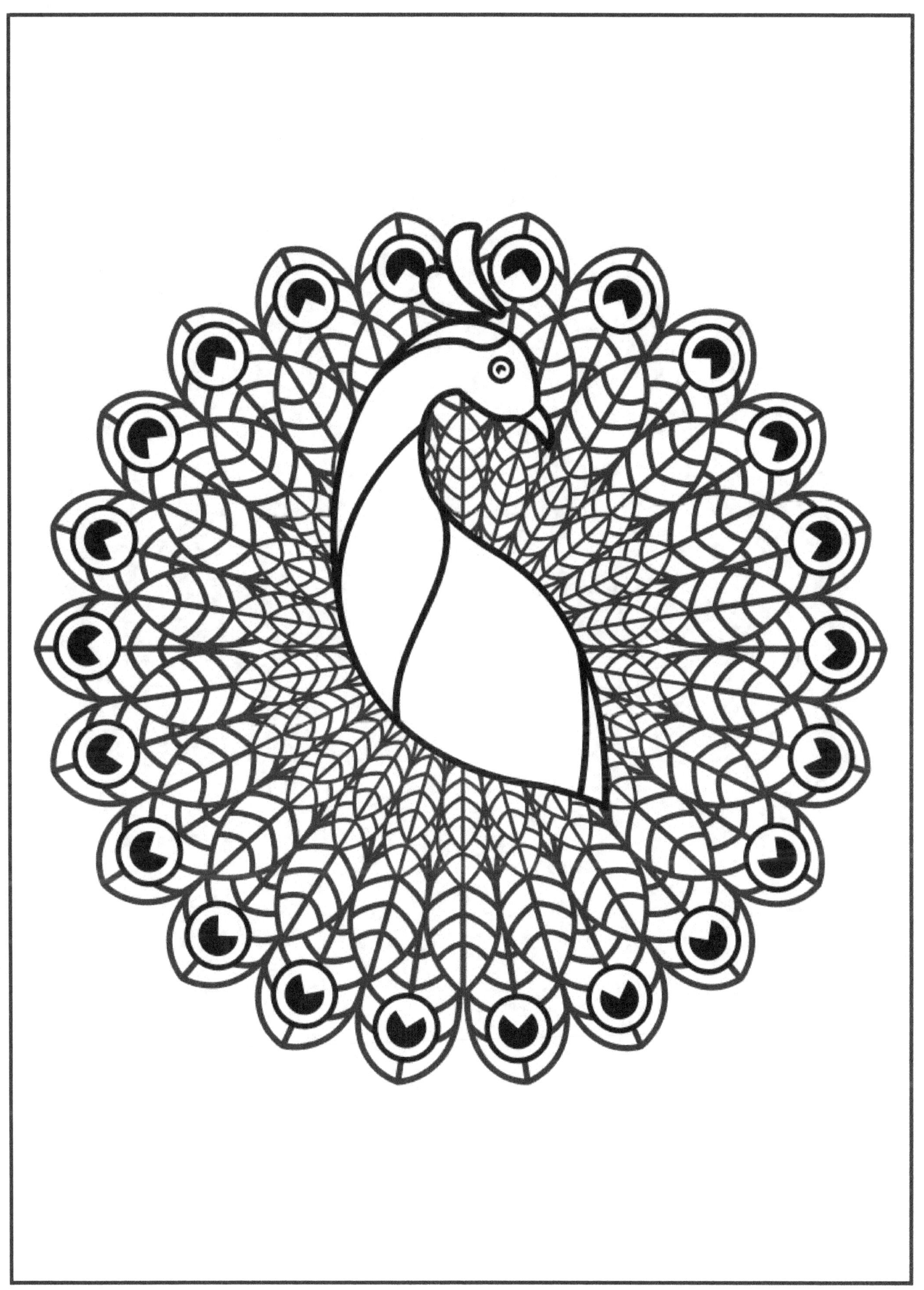

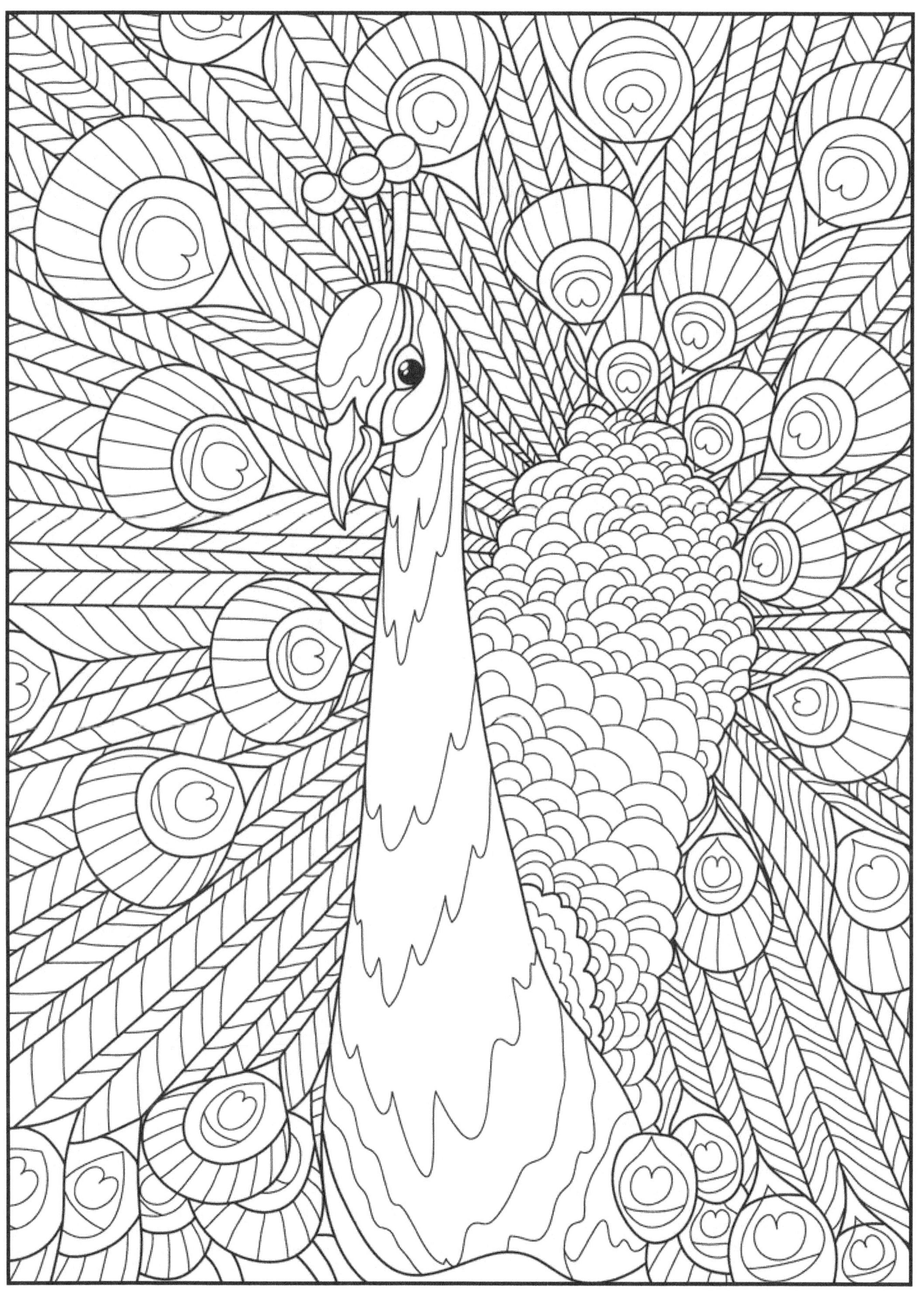

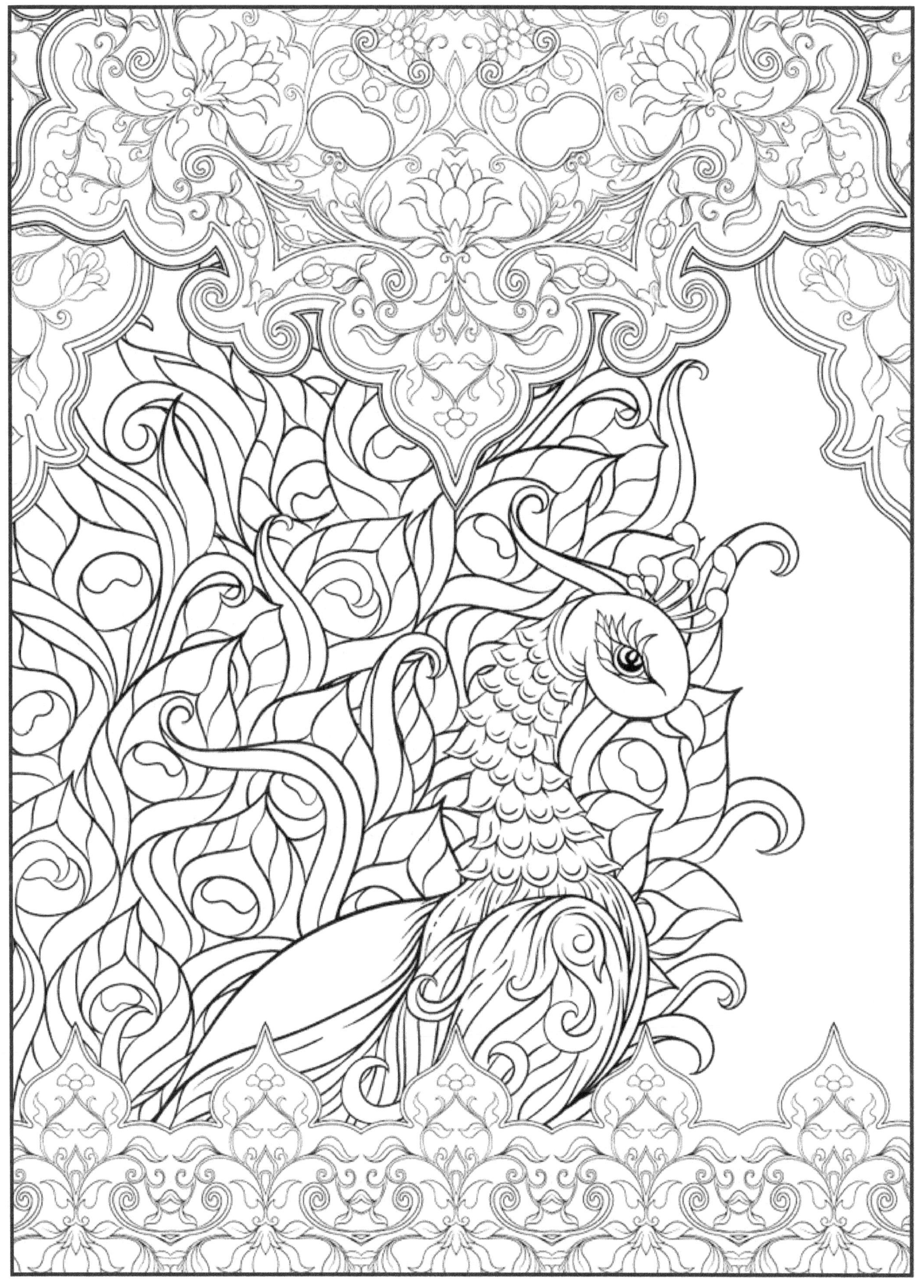

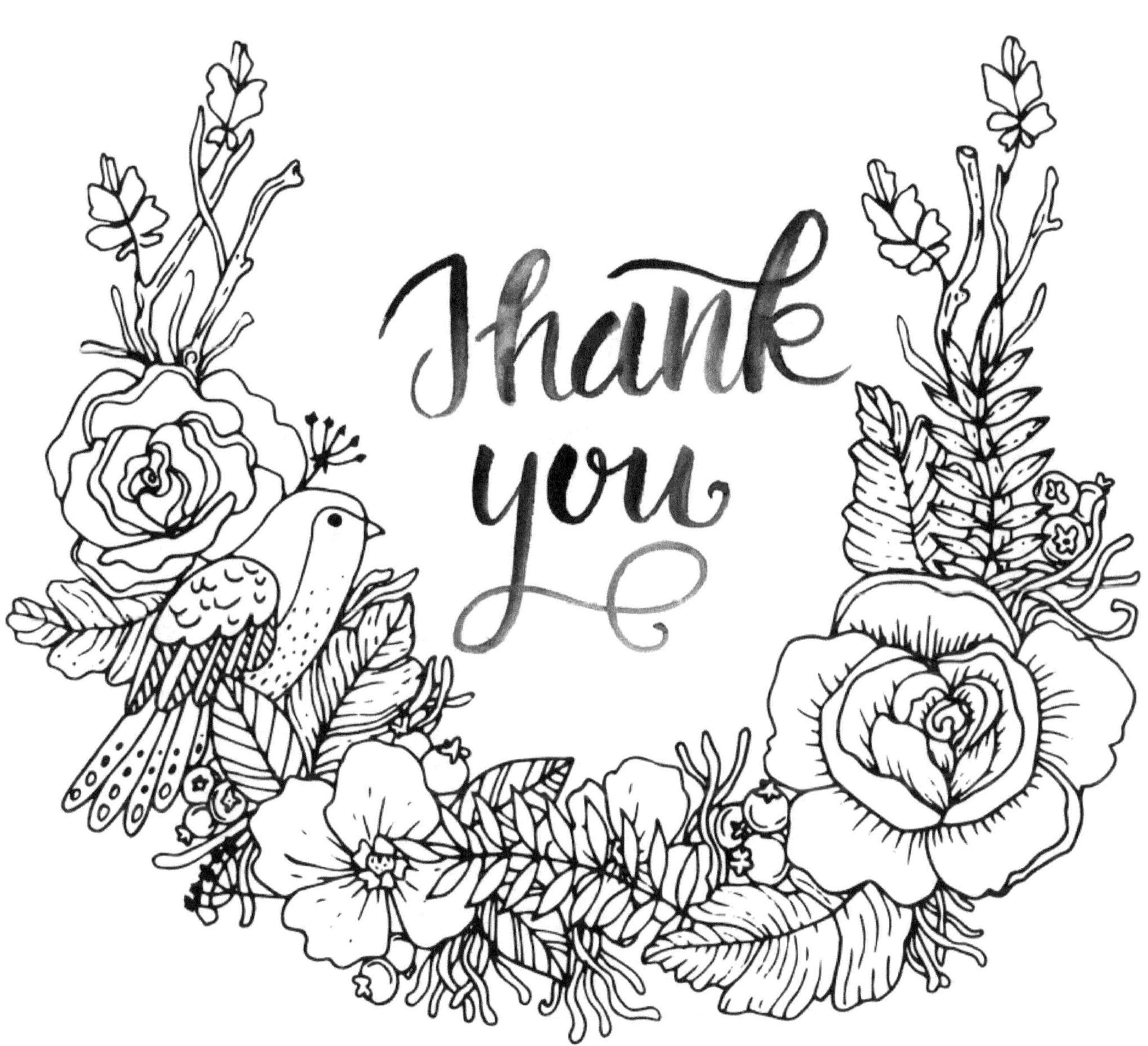
Thank
you

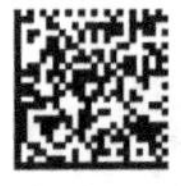